QUESTIONS AND ANSWERS FOR

Practical Cookerv

Ninth Edition

low.

VICT   ESERANI
RO   INTON
DA   SKETT

Hodder & Stoughton

A MEMBER OF THE HODDER HEADLINE

Orders: please contact Bookpoint Ltd, 78 Milton Park, Abingdon, Oxon OX14 4TD.
Telephone: (44) 0235 827720, Fax: (44) 0235 400454. Lines are open from 9.00–6.00, Monday
to Saturday, with a 24-hour message answering service. Email address: orders@bookpoint.co.uk

British Library Cataloguing in Publication Data
A catalogue record for this title is available from The British Library

ISBN 0 340 782439

First published 2000
Impression number 10 9 8 7 6 5 4 3 2 1
Year   2005 2004 2003 2002 2001 2000

Copyright © 2000 Victor Ceserani, Ronald Kinton and David Foskett

Typeset by Transet Limited, Coventry, England
Printed in Great Britain for Hodder and Stoughton Educational, a member of Hodder Headline plc,
338 Euston Road, London NW1 3BH by

CONTENTS

INTRODUCTION

The aim of this book is to assist catering students in their revision by providing questions drawn mainly from the ninth edition of *Practical Cookery* and their own general knowledge of the subject.

Questions are set out in chapters following the *Practical Cookery* format and most chapters commence with a number of short answer questions followed by questions in depth.

The answers are given, mainly in brief outline together with page references to the main text, and follow at the end of each chapter. Many of the answers use key words to assist students to develop a more coherent and comprehensive explanation. Where examples are requested, only specimen answers are given so as to encourage the student to think.

It is the authors' opinion that systematic revision throughout the training years related to the practice of cookery can assist in giving a deeper understanding and knowledge of the subject.

This book should be helpful to those students taking catering courses in schools; BTEC Higher National Diploma; Advanced and Intermediate GNVQ in Hospitality and Catering; NVQ levels 2 and 3 in Food Preparation and Cooking; the examinations of the Hotel, Catering and International Management Association; degree courses; and any others who have an interest in this subject.

The use of *The Theory of Catering* Ninth Edition is recommended.

THE WORKING ENVIRONMENT

CHAPTER 1

Maintain a safe and secure working environment

Read pp 2–3 of *Practical Cookery.*

SHORT QUESTIONS

FIRE PREVENTION

1   Do you know the specific procedures to follow in the event of a fire in your establishment? If so, what are they?

2   Name the three components necessary for a fire to start.

3   Explain the three principal methods to extinguish a fire.

4   What are the correct procedures in the event of a fire in a kitchen?

5   If a fire is spreading in a kitchen what should be done to doors and windows?

6   How frequently should fire alarm bells be tested?

7   What is on all fire extinguishers and displayed by fire hoses?

8   Have you checked which extinguishers to use to put out different fires in your establishment?

9   Have you read the instructions on the extinguisher, understood them and could you competently use it if required?

SUSPICIOUS ITEMS

10   What do you understand to be a suspicious item?

11   Explain why such an item should not be touched.

12   If you become concerned about such an item, what should you do?

13   What specific instructions exist in your establishment?

14 Where is it more likely for such an item to be deposited? Explain why.

15 If you are suspicious about a person, what should you do?

ACCIDENTS

16 In the event of an accident who should be called?

17 If it is a serious accident what is the procedure?

18 Detail the procedure for obtaining an ambulance.

19 Why do accidents usually occur?

20 How can most accidents be prevented?

21 What information should be stated in the Accident Book regarding an accident?

22 Find out who is responsible for the Accident Book in your own establishment and where it is kept.

FIRST AID

23 What is understood by the term first aid?

24 Who should treat a serious injury?

25 How would a first aid box be recognised?

26 To whom would you report if you required first aid in your place of work?

27 State three signs that indicate a person may be about to faint.

28 What is the first aid treatment for a small cut?
sprinkle with salt to disinfect; give a glass of brandy; wash around the cut and apply a waterproof dressing; wrap in a tea towel and send for a doctor

29 Slight burns or scalds should be immersed in:
iced water; warm water; hot running water; cold running water

30 In the event of a person receiving an electric shock what, if possible, should be done first?

31 Name two organisations running first aid courses. Why could attendance at a course be beneficial?

SAFE ENVIRONMENT

32 What is the aim of the Health and Safety at Work Act?

33 What is the employee's responsibility at work regarding safety?

34 What is the employer's responsibility?

35 What is a hazard or a potential hazard?

36 What is the cause of most accidents?

37 Give examples of five hazards.

38 List ten ways to reduce the number of accidents.

SECURE ENVIRONMENT

39 What is understood by a workplace being secure?

40 Who benefits from secure premises?

41 Why is it necessary to have security?

42 What provision should be available for the staff's valuables?

43 What items are most likely to be stolen?

44 What does strict stock control help to prevent?

45 Why is a system necessary regarding keys?

46 What procedure exists in your establishment for lost property?

47 How do you behave if a stranger is being sought on the premises?

Maintain a professional and hygienic appearance

Read p 4 of *Practical Cookery*.

SHORT QUESTIONS

1 Why is it essential to have a professional and hygienic appearance?

2 What standards are expected at your establishment?

3 Define 'professional appearance'.

4 Hygienic appearance indicates high standards of personal hygiene. Explain this statement.

5   Give a description of a person whose appearance is both professional and hygienic.

6   When must a person refrain from handling food?

7   Persons suffering from certain infections must inform their employer who must then report to the medical health officer. What are these infections?

Maintain effective working relationships

Read p 4 of *Practical Cookery*.

SHORT QUESTIONS

1   Why is it essential at work to co-operate with the other members of the team, party or other colleagues?

2   What can you expect from your immediate supervisor in the work environment?

3   A negative attitude is not helpful. What do you understand by being positive?

4   How does communication occur?

5   State how speech can be varied.

6   Listening has to be learnt. Explain this.

7   Give examples of body language.

8   What elements of teamwork are required to make it effective?

Contribute to the development of self and others

Read p 5 of *Practical Cookery*.

SHORT QUESTIONS

1   What should an induction programme include for a new member of staff?

2   How can staff be supportive of each other?

3   Explain how you may develop within the job role.

4   How may you 'know yourself' and create a career in the industry?

Selection, use and care of knives and small equipment

Read p 5 of *Practical Cookery*.

SHORT QUESTIONS

1   Why are blunt knives more likely to cause accidents?

2   State ten rules to be observed with knives.

3   What could be the purpose of colour coding knife handles?

4   Why should the right knife be selected for the correct purpose?

5   Marry up the item with its correct use:

steel	peeling fruit and vegetables
vegetable peeler	trussing poultry
vegetable knife	carving
filleting knife	sharpening
medium large knife	general use, vegetables and fruit
carving knife	filleting fish
boning knife	lifting and holding joints
palette knife	shredding, slicing, chopping
trussing needle	spreading, turning and lifting
fork	butchery

6   Give six examples where extra care needs to be taken when using knives.

7   State two items used for sharpening knives.

8   What may be used to test the sharpness of a knife?

9   Name the uses of the following items:
cooks tongs; vegetable groovers; pastry cutting wheels; vegetable cutters; scissors and secateurs; citrus fruit zesters

Cleaning of cutting equipment

Read p 6 of *Practical Cookery*.

SHORT QUESTIONS

1   Who must not use or clean mechanical machines?

2   Before cleaning electrical cutting machines what must be done?

3   What must be displayed by each machine?

4   Explain the procedure for cleaning power driven machines.

5   Why must extra care be taken when guards are taken off cutting machines when being cleaned?

6   Having completed cleaning and re-assembly, what should be done?

7   When using a mandolin, state the precautions which help prevent accidents.

8   Before cleaning a mandolin, what should be done to the blade?

9   State the care needed when using a grater and why it is necessary to clean it thoroughly.

10   Name the machines which are listed as dangerous.

11   When using liquidisers, what care must be taken?

Maintain clean food production areas, equipment and utensils; food hygiene

Read pp 7–15 of *Practical Cookery*.

SHORT QUESTIONS

1   Name the three interrelated factors in a clean food production environment.

2   What should be available for cleaning the premises?

3   State four essential elements for having good working conditions in a kitchen.

4 How should a kitchen be cleaned?

5 Why should food waste and rubbish not be allowed to accumulate in a kitchen?

6 With what should work surfaces be cleaned?

7 What does correct cleaning and the disposal of waste help prevent?

8 What kind of water should be used for cleaning?

9 Whose instructions should be followed when using equipment?

10 What is the procedure for cleaning large equipment?

11 After cleaning a bain-marie, what must be done?

12 Which small pieces of equipment require particular attention when being cleaned?

13 What general rules would apply to cleaning pots, pans, dishes, etc.?

14 What causes foods to spoil?

15 Describe moulds: what do they require to grow and what prevents them forming?

16 What are yeasts?

17 What are the two kinds of bacteria?

18 How are bacteria conveyed?

19 What is cross contamination?

20 How can salmonella food poisoning be prevented? What is the cause?

21 Salmonella affects which foods?

22 What is the source of salmonella poisoning and which foods are more likely to harbour the bacteria?

23 Clostridium perfringens affects which food? Foods likely to be affected require what kind of cooking?

24 What are the favourable conditions to bacteria?

25 Which foods need extra care?

26 Explain which warm conditions are favourable to the growth of bacteria.

27   State three ways to control bacteria.

28   Which item is exempt from temperature controls?

29   With soup, which is the ideal heat for bacteria to grow – cold; hot; lukewarm; boiling?

30   Do bacteria multiply on dry foods?

31   How is food poisoning recognisable?

32   Give examples of chemicals which may enter food.

33   How may chemical poisoning be prevented?

34   What is understood by infestation?

35   How may infestations be prevented?

36   Left over foods require special care, explain why and what care is necessary?

37   If you are unsure about the freshness or quality of the food, what should you do?

38   What maxim applies especially to left over foods?

SHORT QUESTIONS – ANSWERS

FIRE PREVENTION

1   check within your premises   *p3 PC*

2   fuel – something to burn; air – oxygen to sustain combustion; heat – gas, electricity etc.   *p2 PC*

3   starving – removing the fuel; smothering – removing the air; cooling – removing the heat   *p2 PC*

4   call the fire brigade; don't panic; warn others; don't jeopardise safety of others or self; follow fire instructions; use appropriate extinguisher; close doors and windows; turn off gas, electricity and fans   *p2 PC*

5   close them

6   four times a year

7   instructions on how to use them

8   if not, you should do so

9   ideally, you should have a demonstration in its use

SUSPICIOUS ITEMS

10   any items (box, bag, holdall etc.) in full view, hidden or partially hidden in a strange or unusual place   *p2 PC*

11   it may explode or cause a fire, and death or injury could result

12   do not panic; warn others in the vicinity; do not touch the item and warn others not to do so; inform employers immediately; move to a safe place   *p2 PC*

13   find out from your employers their specific instructions

14   in places which may be left unattended for some time, since there is less chance of the person being seen depositing the item and less chance of it being found

15   ensure that you can give an accurate description of the suspicious person, and immediately inform senior staff

ACCIDENTS

16   the person responsible for first aid   *p2 PC*

17   an ambulance should be obtained

18   dial 999, state you require an ambulance; state the exact location of the incident; give the address and phone number of the location; describe the accident – if a heart attack is suspected say so immediately; indicate the age of casualty or casualties

19   due to excessive haste; distraction; failure to apply safety rules
                    p2 PC

20   by concentrating on the job in hand; by being safety conscious; using tools and equipment correctly at all times; by taking care

21   name of person or persons involved; time, date and place of accident; cause of accident; treatment given on the spot; where sent, name of hospital; names of any witnesses   *p2 PC*

22   check with the person to whom you are responsible

FIRST AID

23 treatment to an injury on the spot. Preferably given by a trained first aider at the work place   *p2 PC*

24 a nurse or doctor

25 by the sign of a white cross on a green background

26 check this in your establishment

27 whiteness, giddiness, sweating

28 wash and apply waterproof dressing

29 cold running water

30 turn off the current

31 Red Cross, St John's or St Andrews', a course would provide up to date information, practical experience and thus enable confident and correct first aid to be given

SAFE ENVIRONMENT

32 to extend the protection of the law to all employees and employers; to increase awareness of safety at work, both employees and employers   *p3 PC*

33 to take reasonable care to prevent injury to self or others; to co-operate with employers so as to comply with the law; to refrain from misusing and interfering with anything provided for health and safety   *p3 PC*

34 to provide safe and healthy premises and equipment; provide supervision, information and training; issue a written statement of safety policy to employees; consult with employees' safety representative and establish a safety committee   *p3 PC*

35 anything which may cause an accident or an injury

36 slips, trips and falls; incorrect lifting; burns, cuts and scalds

37 power plug 'on' when cleaning electrical equipment; trailing electrical flexes; faulty sockets; overloading plugs; failure to replace lighting bulbs or tubes; not using steps; having wet hands when handling plugs; gas pilot not alight; main gas not igniting   *p3 PC*

38 floors in good repair and free from obstacles; spillage cleaned at once; warning notices of slippery floors; guards on machines; extra care when cleaning machinery; one person to operate machine; use machine with care; use only sound cloths when handling hot pans etc.; pan handles must not protrude; correctly lift heavy items; use trolley for heavy items; never place knives in sinks; use knives with care and correctly; signs must indicate hazardous machines; protective clothing must be worn so as to protect; footwear must be in a good state of repair

SECURE ENVIRONMENT

39   premises free from unauthorised persons, where the possessions of those using the establishment are safe   *p3 PC*

40   staff, customers and management

41   to prevent crime of any kind e.g. stealing, mugging

42   lockers

43   valuable items; personal possessions, e.g. jewellery, watches; alcoholic liquor; expensive foods; cash

44   stock control reduces the possibility that the stealing of stock goes unnoticed; awareness of control will limit the opportunies for theft

45   to enable only authorised persons to use them

46   check the procedure in your establishment

47   with care; do not endanger yourself, inform your supervisor

Maintain a professional and hygienic appearance

SHORT QUESTIONS — **ANSWERS**

1   in the self interest of the individual – gives confidence, pride and creates a good impression to others   *p4 PC*

2   do you find the standards are maintained?

3   one whose appearance is indicated by their clothing, clean and correctly worn, and themselves – clean hands, finger nails, shaven, neat hair, etc.

4   personal hygiene standards include daily bathing; washing hands after use of toilet; not handling hair, mouth or nose; not coughing or sneezing over food; not smoking in food areas; tasting food with a clean spoon; not sitting on work surfaces

5   one having the right attitude to the profession indicated by cleanliness, neatness, keenness, willingness, interest and a caring manner

6   when suffering from vomiting; diarrhoea; sore throat; head cold

7   sufferers or carriers of typhoid; para-typhoid; salmonella; staphylococcal infection   *p4 PC*

Maintain effective working relationships

SHORT QUESTIONS — ANSWERS _____

1   to enable customers or consumers to receive the goods and service to their satisfaction; for employers to continue in business and develop; for employees to obtain job satisfaction   *p4 PC*

2   to be given instructions, guidance and constructive criticism; you may also receive encouragement

3   to look on the bright side; to try to see the good points; to be hopeful

4   through speech, by listening, by body language

5   by volume; pitch; tone; pace

6   it is necessary to pay attention; to concentrate; to maintain eye contact; to show interest; to note the essentials so as to take action correctly   *p4 PC*

7   e.g. facial expression; gestures; gaze; proximity   *p4 PC*

8   same objective; each one pulling their weight; supportive of one another; being co-operative to each other; sharing success and failure; helping each other   *p5 PC*

Contribute to the development of self and others

SHORT QUESTIONS — ANSWERS _____

1   a briefing about the organisation or company; conditions of employment; an organisation chart; fire and evacuation procedures; first aid procedures; an introduction to members of staff and instructions on what, how, when and where the work has to be done

2   knowing each other's skills and assisting others to acquire them; by generating commitment and keenness; establishing standards of quality, timing, good work practices; developing a good co-operative attitude to one another   *p5 PC*

3   by assessing one's good and weak points; by obtaining good constructive advice; practising skills and working hard; ensuring that personal hygiene and appearance are exemplary, and that attitude to work, colleagues and employers is always courteous and constructive   *p5 PC*

4   by taking notice of constructive comments by colleagues and supervisors

Selection, use and care of knives and small equipment

SHORT QUESTIONS — ANSWERS _____

1   more pressure has to be used, therefore the knife may slip, and there is more likely to be an accident   *p5 PC*

2   knife point down; flat on table; not over table edge; correct knife for right purpose; kept sharp; wiped after use, handles kept clean; not left in sink; not mis-used; no distraction when being used; wash, dry and put safely away   *p5 PC*

3   to prevent cross contamination

4   each knife has been so designed for a specific use

5   steel – sharpening
    vegetable peeler – peeling fruit and vegetables
    vegetable knife – general use for fruit and vegetables
    filleting knife – filleting fish
    medium large knife – shredding, slicing, chopping
    carving knife – carving
    boning knife – butchery
    palette knife – spreading, turning items over, lifting
    trussing needle – trussing poultry

6   cutting sideways; using a trussing needle; when chopping; scoring
    pork rind; using frozen foods; controlling a large knife

7   steel, carborundum stone

8   skin of a tomato

9   tongs – turning and lifting foods
    groovers – for ornamental use, decorative
    cutting wheels – cutting pasta and other pastry shapes
    vegetable cutters – scoop shaped oval or round balls
    scissors and secateurs – trimming fish; cutting poultry
    zesters – to obtain thin ribbon of skin of citrus fruit

Cleaning of cutting equipment

SHORT QUESTIONS – ANSWERS _____

1   persons under 18 years of age   *p6 PC*

2   turn off the electricity and remove plug   *p6 PC*

3   instructions on its use and safety precautions   *p6 PC*

4   switch off and remove plug; remove food particles; clean
    thoroughly; rinse and dry; reassemble and test

5   blades when exposed can be very dangerous and cause severe
    cuts

6   plug in, switch on and check that machine is correctly reassembled

7   take extra care, make certain no part of hand or fingers come into
    contact with the blade, do not exert excess pressure   *p6 PC*

8   the blade must be closed

9 ensure hand or fingers do not come into contact with the grater; to make certain no food is left in the holes

10 mincing machines; bowl type choppers; dough mixers; food mixers with attachments for various cuts; pie and tart machines; vegetable slicing, potato chipping and circular knife slicing machines

11 cool hot liquids, make sure lid is firmly on

Maintain clean food production areas, equipment and utensils; food hygiene

SHORT QUESTIONS – ANSWERS

1 personal hygiene; kitchen hygiene; food hygiene

2 brushes; clothes; detergent and bactericide; plenty of hot water

3 adequate lighting; ventilation; easily cleanable; well maintained

4 systematically; efficiently; organised according to a rota

5 to prevent the accumulation of bacteria, smells and pests

6 hot water containing detergent   *p7 PC*

7 accidents; contamination; fire hazard; pest infestation; unpleasant smells; pollution of the environment

8 hot water   *p7 PC*

9 manufacturer's

10 turn off fuel supply; wash with hot detergent water; remove any food; rinse; dry; test   *p7 PC*

11 close the tap

12 sieves; conical strainers etc.; items which have small holes which may contain food particles

13 soak if necessary, clean in very hot water with detergent, rinse, dry

14 micro organisms

15 like whiskers; require warmth, moisture, air, darkness and a food to grow on; cold dry storage   *p7 PC*

16 single cell organisms which grow on moist, sweet foods, which are
destroyed by heat *p7 PC*

17 helpful and harmful *p7 PC*

18 hands, cuts, sores, burns, coughs and sneezes; other foods,
unclean equipment surfaces; air, water, insects and birds, vermin,
poor waste disposal *p9 PC*

19 unaffected food becoming contaminated by transference of
bacteria from another item or medium

20 good standards of personal hygiene; elimination of insects and
rodents; thorough washing after handling raw poultry; using
shellfish from reputable sources; not allowing carriers of the
disease to handle food *p9 PC*
It is caused by actual bacteria

21 poultry; meat; eggs; raw foods; shellfish *p9 PC*

22 caused by poisons produced in the food by the bacteria. Foods
handled a lot e.g. brawn, pressed beef, pies *p9 PC*

23 raw meat and poultry; they require thorough cooking *p9 PC*

24 warmth; moisture; time; a suitable food *p9 PC*

25 stocks, sauces, gravies, soups; meat and meat products; milk and
milk products, egg and egg products; foods which are handled;
foods which are reheated *p9 PC*

26 temperature between 7°C (45°F) and 63°C (145°F); body
temperature; badly ventilated kitchens; luke warm water/warm
weather; insufficient heating of refrigerated foods *p9 PC*

27 prevent bacteria from spreading by keeping foods covered;
preventing cross contamination; using colour coded boards and
knives; correct storage, frequent hand washing *p10 PC*

do not keep foods in the temperature danger zone longer than
necessary: that is between 8°C–63°C (48°F–145°F)

killing bacteria by subjecting it to 77°C for 30 seconds; using
certain chemicals.

28 canned foods unless stated otherwise on the can

29 lukewarm

30 no

31   by stomach pains, diarrhoea and vomiting, developing within
         1–16 hours after eating affected food

32   arsenic; lead; zinc; copper; rat poison   *p14 PC*

33   properly maintained equipment; obtaining foods from reliable
         sources; taking care in the use of rat poison etc.   *p14 PC*

34   premises invaded by rodents, e.g. rats and mice, and insects e.g.
         flies, cockroaches, beetles, silver fish   *p14 PC*

35   no structural defects so that rodents can get in; screens on
         windows to keep out insects and cockroaches; having hygienic
         conditions for stores and waste   *p14 PC*

36   reheating must be thorough; as quickly as possible; with the
         minimum of handling; not held at a low temperature; in order to
         reduce the opportunity for bacteria to multiply   *p15 PC*

37   'if in doubt throw it out'

NUTRITION AND HEALTHY EATING

CHAPTER 2

Read pp 16–21 of *Practical Cookery*.

SHORT QUESTIONS

1   What is a food?

2   What is nutrition?

3   Name the energy giving foods.

4   Name the body building foods.

5   What are the protective foods?

6   Why is water an essential nutrient?

7   Explain a balanced diet.

8   What changes are needed to produce a healthy diet?

9   Specify eight points which are guidelines to a healthy diet.

10   How may customer requirements be met relating to their weight?

11   What is a nutritional analysis of a recipe?

12   What do kilocalories or kilojoules indicate?

13   How many portions of fruit and vegetables are needed per individual per day?

14   Which is the healthiest: coconut oil or rape seed oil?

15   State three basic qualities which ensure enjoyment of food.

16   Fill in the blanks:

　　e.g. natural yoghurt in place of cream;
　　　　 . . . in place of animal fat;
　　　　 instead of white flour use . . .;
　　　　 skimmed milk instead of . . .;
　　　　 . . . in place of full fat cheese

17   What do you understand by the term pathogens?

QUESTIONS IN DEPTH

1   a   When considering a healthy diet what are the chief ingredients that should be used in moderation?
    b   Name the four medical conditions that can develop if we do not follow a healthy diet.
2   a   Discuss six ways in which nutritional analysis can be used?
    b   What does the following nutritional analysis for one portion of breadcrumbed veal, ham and cheese escalope reveal?
            627kcals – 48.1g fat of which 16.3g is saturated;
            12.0g carbohydrate of which 1.3g is sugars, 37.1g
            protein, 0.7g fibre
    c   State the format for nutritional information.

SHORT QUESTIONS – ANSWERS

1   a liquid or solid which provides the body with material for heat and energy, growth and repair, to regulate body processes

2   the study of nutrients, that is those substances in food which assist in keeping the body healthy   *p17 PC*

3   sugars; starches; fats   *p17–18 PC*

4   animal protein – meat, fish, eggs, milk, cheese; vegetable protein – peas, beans, lentils, nuts, cereals   *p17–18 PC*

5   mineral elements and vitamins   *p17–18 PC*

6   it cleanses the body and assists in keeping the body healthy *p18 PC*

7   a balanced diet is one that provides adequate amounts of the nutrients   *p20 PC*

8   for most people, a reduction in the intake of sugar, fat and salt

9   enjoy food; have a variety of different foods; eat the right amount; have plenty of food rich in starch and fibre; limit the amount of fat; limit the amount of sugar; consider intake of minerals and vitamins; drink only sensible amounts of alcohol, if any   *p20 PC*

10 offer a selection of items so that they may choose what suits their diets

11   a breakdown of what the dish consists of; protein, fat, carbohydrate etc.

12   the energy content

13   five

14   rape seed oil

15   inviting; appetising; pleasant taste

16   vegetable oil; wholemeal flour; full cream milk; low fat cheese

17   harmful germs (disease-forming organisms)

QUESTIONS IN DEPTH – OUTLINE ANSWERS _____

1   a   fat; sugar; fibre; salt
    b   obesity; heart disease; some cancers; some diseases of the digestive system
2   a   menu labelling e.g. traffic light scheme; recipe cards, customer hand-outs; posters, leaflets; articles for media; healthier standard recipes; specific marketing initiatives e.g. healthy eating days
    b   1 portion provides – state per portion or per recipe; express energy content as kilocalories or kilojoules; total fat listed with saturated fat; need to aim for more starchy carbohydrate and less sugar; protein content; fibre content   *C*
    c   a working man may need 2,600–2,900kcals daily; maximum recommended amount of fat for average person 80–85g; starch and sugar content of dish low; a working man may need about 75g protein daily; negligible fibre content

METHODS OF COOKERY

CHAPTER 3

Read pp 23–42 of *Practical Cookery.*

SHORT QUESTIONS

1 What is the effect of heat on food in the following?
    protein; vitamin D; vitamin C

2 What is the effect of dry and moist heat on the carbohydrates starch and sugar?

3 State three important points to be observed if the maximum vitamin C is to be retained when cooking vegetables.

4 List twelve methods or processes of cooking food.

5 Give a definition for boiling.

6 Give examples of the following foods cooked by boiling:
    fish; vegetables; meat

7 What particular consideration applies when boiling salted or pickled meats, e.g. silverside of beef?

8 Approximately how long per ½kg (1lb) is allowed for boiling meat?
    15 minutes; 20 minutes; 25 minutes; 30 minutes

9 Vegetables grown above the ground are cooked in which of the following?
    cold water; warm water; hot water; boiling water

10 Vegetables such as turnips and cauliflower should be boiled gently otherwise they will:
    taste strong; lose colour; become mashed; lose flavour

11 State three advantages of boiling.

12 Name four essential safety practices when boiling.

13 Define poaching.

14 Name three different foods, with examples of dishes, which may be cooked by poaching.

15 **a** Specify two points which must apply when poaching food.
b To which food, when poached, do the general rules not apply?

16 Give a definition for stewing.

17 Why does the stewing of meat have nutritional advantages?

18 Which of the following meats is suitable for stewing?
coarser types; tender cuts; prime joints; young carcass

19 Name a dish of each of the following cooked by stewing:
a meat; **b** poultry; **c** vegetables

20 State four safety points to be observed when stewing.

21 Give a definition for braising.

22 **a** What are the two methods of braising?
b Give an example of a dish cooked by each.

23 What is meant by each of the following terms associated with braising?
a sealing; **b** marinating; **c** sweating; **d** browning

24 Why is it necessary to use a pan with a tight fitting lid when braising?
to protect the contents; to prevent coloration; to prevent evaporation; to increase coloration

25 What is the ideal oven temperature for braising?

26 Meat may be marinaded before braising in a mixture of which of the following?
wine, vegetables and herbs; stock, vegetables and herbs; vinegar, vegetables and spices; wine, herbs and spices

27 Name four vegetables which may be braised.

28 Briefly describe two different ways of steaming food.

29 Give the definition for steaming.

30 State three points of safety to be observed when steaming foods.

31 Name four foods suitable for cooking by steaming.

32 What is meant by cooking sous-vide?

33 State three advantages of sous-vide.

34 Name two foods suitable for cooking sous-vide.

35 Explain the difference between baking and roasting.

36 How does the heat of the oven cook a baked jacket potato?

37 Why are egg custards cooked in a bain-marie?

38 What is toad in the hole?

  sausage in batter; sausage roll; a hot dog; a ham roll

39 Why is time and temperature control so essential when baking?

40 What is meant by 'recovery time' when using baking ovens?

41 State four general rules for baking.

42 Define oven roasting.

43 What is meant by basting meat?
  inserting pieces of fat meat; batting out with a cutlet bat; spooning the cooking fat over the meat; covering with a slice of fat

44 Why is basting necessary?
  to flavour the fat; to prevent drying; to colour gravy; to increase evaporation

45 Beef when roasted should be well done: true/false.

46 Why is it essential to commence roasting in a pre-heated oven?

47 What is the difference between a conventional general purpose oven and a convection oven?

48 When roasting pork how much time should you allow, approximately?
  25 minutes per ½kg and 25 minutes over; 20 minutes per ½kg and 20 minutes over; 15 minutes per ½kg and 15 minutes over; 10 minutes per ½kg and 10 minutes over

49 **a** What are the approximate cooking times per ½kg (1lb) for roasting beef and lamb?
  b Name two vegetables which may be roasted.

50 What is the purpose of a meat thermometer?

51 Why should joints of meat or poultry be roasted on a trivet or grid?

52   A fast method of cooking by radiated heat describes which method of cookery?

53   Which is the odd one out, and why?
       cooking on a grill; cooking under a salamander; cooking on a spit; cooking between grill bars?

54   **a**   Describe three different ways of grilling food.
     b   Give a menu example for each.

55   Why are grill bars pre-heated and brushed with oil before use?

56   What are the nutritional effects of grilling?

57   Name four terms which describe the degrees of grilling steaks.

58   **a**   Tomatoes and mushrooms are grilled under the . . . ?
     b   Name four foods suitable for cooking on a griddle.

59   Why are certain foods grilled on trays?
       to improve the flavour; to prevent them falling between grill bars; to cook them more slowly; to colour them more evenly

60   Define two methods of frying.

61   Explain the meaning of the term *sauté* when applied to cooking poultry or meat.

62   What is meant by the term *meunière* and to what type of food is it usually applied?

63   Define stir frying.

64   What are the effects of shallow frying on food?

65   Give eight points essential to ensure safe deep frying.

66   Why is it necessary to coat most foods which are to be deep fried?

67   Name three coatings which may be used to coat foods for deep frying.

68   Which of the following fruits are suitable for coating in batter and deep frying?
       bananas; apples; pineapples; strawberries; cherries; oranges?

69   Why is it essential to strain deep fat after each use?

70   Explain the principle of microwave cookery.

71   Can a microwave oven be used for defrosting food?

72 What is standing time related to microwave cookery?

73 Give two major disadvantages of microwave cookery.

74 Give advantages of microwave cookery.

75 Why is a microwave oven so useful for reheating food?

76 Define pot-roasting.

77 Give three examples of food that may be pot-roasted.

78 When pot-roasting, what are the food juices and the bed of roots used for after the food is cooked?

79 **a** Why is presentation so important in the appearance of cold food?
    b Give three basic principles to achieve attractive presentation.

80 Where should cold food be kept before, during and after assembling before final garnishing?

QUESTIONS IN DEPTH

1   **a** List 12 methods or processes of cooking food. With the minimum of repetition suggest two different foods suitable for cooking by each method.
    b Write each dish as it would appear on a menu.

BOILING

2   **a** Define boiling as a method of cookery and name four liquids in which foods can be boiled.
    b Give two menu examples of each of the following foods cooked by boiling:
          fish; meat; poultry; vegetables
    c **i** What are the advantages of boiling related to meats and poultry
         ii What is the approximate cooking time per $\frac{1}{2}$kg (1lb) for boiling salted or pickled meat?
    d Give the four safety points associated with boiling, and explain their importance.

POACHING

3   **a** Define poaching as a method of cookery and its purpose.
    b What are the two methods of poaching food? Give two menu examples for each.

   c What do the following techniques mean?
          cutting and tying; folding; draining; reducing for sauce
   d Why are time and temperature important when poaching
          food?

STEWING

4 **a** Define stewing and its purpose as a method of cookery.
     b What gives the thickened consistency of a stew?
     c What are the effects of stewing?
     d Suggest two dishes from each of the following cooked by
            stewing:
            meat; poultry; vegetables

5 **a** What are the advantages of stewing?
     b What are the safety rules that should be observed?
     c What is the procedure for care and cleanliness of pans used for
            stewing?
     d Name four items of equipment that can be used for stewing.

BRAISING

6 **a** Give a definition for braising and its purpose.
     b Describe the two methods of braising and give two different
            menu examples for each.
     c What are the effects and advantages of braising?
     d Explain the following techniques:
            a sealing;   **b** larding;   **c** marinating;   **d** sweating

STEAMING

7 **a** Define steaming and state its purpose.
     b Describe the various methods of steaming.
     c What are the effects and advantages of steaming?
     d Give two menu examples of food cooked by steaming from
            the following:
            fish; meat; vegetables; sweets

8 **a** Discuss the method and advantages of vacuum cooking in a
            pouch known as sous-vide.
     b What are the essential safety precautions to be observed when
            using steamers?
     c What are the following techniques?
            i moulding;   **ii** traying-up;   **iii** loading;   **iv** preparation
            of container

BAKING

9   **a** State the definition and purpose of baking.
    b What are the methods and effects of baking?
    c What are the advantages of baking?
    d Describe the following techniques:
       i marking; **ii** brushing; **iii** cooling; **iv** finishing;
       v recovery time; **vi** dusting

ROASTING

10 **a** Define roasting and explain the various methods.
    b What are the effects and advantages of roasting?
    c How are time and temperature controlled?
    d What are the safety points when roasting?

GRILLING

11 **a** Give the definition for grilling and explain the various
       methods and the effects.
    b Explain in detail the degrees of grilling meat and describe the
       appearance of the juice issuing from the meat.
    c Give two menu examples for each of the following foods
       cooked by grilling:
          fish; meat; vegetables; savoury
    d List the general rules for efficient grilling and the safety
       precautions that should be observed.

SHALLOW FRYING

12 **a** State the definition and explain the methods of shallow frying.
    b Give the effects and advantages of shallow frying and two
       menu examples for each of the following foods:
          eggs; fish; meat; poultry; vegetables; sweets
    c Suggest three items of small equipment and two items of large
       equipment suitable for shallow frying.
    d Give the safety rules essential for shallow frying.

DEEP FRYING

13 **a** Give definition and the methods of deep frying.
    b What are the effects and advantages?
    c Explain in detail the requirements for efficient and safe deep
       frying.
    d Give a menu description for ten deep fried foods.

MICROWAVE

14 a Define in detail the principles of the microwave as used in an oven and the various types of food that can be cooked.

 b List the advantages and disadvantages.

 c List the special points for attention when cooking and factors which affect efficient cooking.

 d How does microwaved food differ in appearance and what is the difference in equipment used?

COLD PREPARATION

15 a Correct hygiene practices regarding personal habits, food and equipment are essential at all times, particularly when dealing with cold food. Summarise these hygiene practices.

 b Discuss the preparation for cold work.

 c What should be the characteristics of cold food?

 d Suggest six appetising cold buffet dishes.

SHORT QUESTIONS – ANSWERS _____

1 coagulates; not destroyed; easily lost (water soluble)   *p23 PC*

2 starch – dry heat causes colour changes
            moist heat causes grains to soften and swell
    sugar – dry heat causes caramelisation
            moist heat dissolves   *p23 PC*

3 do not soak in water; cook in small quantities; cook quickly and do not overcook; cut at the last minute   *p24 PC*

4 boiling; poaching; stewing; braising; steaming; baking; roasting; grilling; deep and shallow frying; paperbag; microwave; pot-roasting

5 cooking in liquid at boiling point (100°C)   *p24 PC*

6 e.g. turbot: salmon; cod
        cabbage; carrots; swedes
        silverside of beef; bacon; leg of mutton

7 may require soaking depending on the salt content

8 30 minutes to the lb plus 30 minutes

9 boiling water

10 become mashed

11   older, tougher, cheaper meat and poultry made palatable and
      digestible; nutritious stock results; labour saving   *pp24–25 PC*

12   correct size of container; move pans carefully; position of handles;
      care when handling boiling liquid   *pp24–25 PC*

13   cooking in minimum liquid just below boiling point   *p26 PC*

14   e.g. eggs – poached eggs on spinach with cheese sauce
           fish – poached Finnan haddock
           fruit – assorted fruit compote

15   a   temperature control; strict control of cooking time
      b   eggs   *p26 PC*

16   slow cooking of food cut in pieces, cooked in minimum liquid
                                                                   p26 PC

17   slow cooking converts meat connective tissue into gelatinous
      substance so that fibres fall apart and become digestible protein
      coagulated but not toughened; collagen forms into gelatine
                                                                   pp26–27 PC

18   coarser types

19   e.g. **a** Irish stew;   **b** chicken fricassée;   **c** ratatouille

20   e.g. suitable sized pans; care when removing hot pans from oven
      and when removing pan lids; sprinkle of flour on hot pans when
      off stove   *p28 PC*

21   cooking in liquid or sauce in covered pan in oven.   *p28 PC*

22   a   brown; white   *pp28–29 PC*
      b   e.g. beef olives; braised celery

23   a   application of heat to meat surface to prevent escape of juices;
      b   steeping in richly spiced liquid for flavour;
      c   extraction of flavour without coloration;
      d   colouring a surface by application of heat   *pp28–29 PC*

24   to prevent evaporation

25   160°C (gas mark 3)

26   wine, vegetables and herbs

27   e.g. onions, leeks, endive, celery

28   e.g. atmospheric or low pressure; high pressure in purpose built
      equipment   *pp29–30 PC*

29   cooking under various degrees of steam pressure (moist heat) at or above atmospheric pressure   *pp29–30 PC*

30   e.g. allow steam pressure to reduce before opening door; take care not to scald oneself when opening door; check water level and ball valve arms where applicable   *p30 PC*

31   e.g. potatoes, vegetables, fish, sponge puddings

32   food contained in vacuum-sealed plastic pouches cooked by steam   *p29 PC*

33   e.g. minimal change of texture and weight loss; food cooks in own natural juices; uniformity of standard   *p29 PC*

34   e.g. cuts of fish; breast of chicken   *p29 PC*

35   baking cooks by dry oven heat; roasting cooks by moist oven heat   *p31 PC*

36   steam builds up from the water content in the potato and combines with dry heat to cook it   *p31 PC*

37   to modify the heat, cook more slowly and lessen the risk of overcooking the egg mixture   *p31 PC*

38   sausage cooked in Yorkshire pudding batter

39   unless ovens are heated to the correct temperature before foods are inserted they will be spoiled   *p31 PC*

40   time required for ovens to reach the correct temperature before cooking a further batch of food   *p31 PC*

41   e.g. accuracy in weighing and measuring; temperature control; utilise oven space efficiently; correct preparation of trays and moulds   *p31 PC*

42   cooking in dry heat with oil or fat in an oven or on a spit   *p32 PC*

43   spooning the cooking fat over the meat   *p32 PC*

44   to prevent drying

45   false, it is usually cooked medium

46   to seal the surface protein and prevent escape of natural juices

47   air circulation – in a conventional oven the temperature varies in different parts of the oven. In a convection oven the powered fan gives an even temperature all over

48 25 minutes per ½kg plus 25 minutes   *p32 PC*

49 a   beef 15 minutes; lamb 20 minutes   *p32 PC*
     b   e.g. potatoes; parsnips

50 to determine the exact temperature in the centre of the meat
being roasted   *p32 PC*

51 to raise the joint from the fat in the roasting tray and prevent it
frying

52 grilling   *p33 PC*

53 on a spit – this is roasting; the other three are methods of grilling

54 a   over heat; under heat; between heat   *pp33–34 PC*
     b   e.g. a grilled steak; mushrooms; toasted sandwich

55 to prevent food sticking   *pp33–34 PC*

56 because of the speed of cooking there is maximum retention of
nutrients and flavour   *p35 PC*

57 rare; under done; just done; well done   *p34 PC*

58 a   Salamander
     b   e.g. hamburgers; sausages; eggs; pancakes

59 to prevent them falling between grill bars

60 shallow – cooking food in a small quantity of pre-heated oil or fat;
deep – cooking in pre-heated deep oil or fat   *pp35–36 PC*

61 small pieces of poultry or meat rapidly cooked on both sides in a
sauté or frying pan   *p36 PC*

62 meunière is the cooking of floured fish in shallow fat or oil on
both sides and finishing with lemon juice, nut-brown butter and
chopped parsley   *p36 PC*

63 fast frying of small pieces of food in a little oil in a wok or frying
pan   *p37 PC*

64 the high temperature produces almost instant coagulation of
surface protein of the food thus retaining natural juices   *p37 PC*

65 e.g. do not over-fill deep fat fryer; dry food thoroughly; do not
overload deep fat fryer; place food in carefully   *p39 PC*

66 protect food surface from excess heat; prevent escape of moisture
and nutrients; modify penetration of intense heat   *p38 PC*

67   milk and flour; egg and crumbs; batter

68   bananas; apples; pineapple

69   food particles remaining in fat will brown and spoil fresh food
     being fried   *p38 PC*

70   high frequency power from a magnetron develops microwaves at a
     high frequency which activate water molecules or particles of food
     and agitates them causing heat by friction   *p39 PC*

71   yes

72   removing certain foods, e.g. scrambled eggs, while underdone as
     they will complete cooking in standing time   *p42 PC*

73   not suitable for all foods, limited oven space   *p40 PC*

74   e.g. time saving, economical on energy   *p40 PC*

75   because the food is heated quickly

76   cooking on bed of root vegetables in a covered pan   *p33 PC*

77   e.g. chicken; fillet of beef; pheasant

78   the basis of a sauce to coat or accompany the food   *p33 PC*

79   **a**   should stimulate the appetite
     b   clean and fresh appearance; colourful presentation; not over
          decorated or handled

80   in a cool place, cold room or refrigerator

QUESTIONS IN DEPTH – OUTLINE ANSWERS _____

1   **a Methods   Suitable foods**   **b Menu examples**

Methods	Suitable foods	Menu examples
boiling	beef silverside	boiled silverside of beef, dumplings, onions, carrots
poaching	eggs	poached eggs with cheese sauce
stewing	lamb	lamb stew with vegetables
braising	duck	braised duck and peas
steaming	potatoes	new jersey potatoes
baking	apples	baked apple dumpling
roasting	pheasant	roast pheasant
grilling	mushrooms	mushrooms on toast
shallow frying	trout	shallow fried trout with almonds

deep frying	cod fillet	fried fillet of cod in batter
paper	veal chop	veal chop in a bag
microwave	smoked haddock	smoked haddock
pot-roasting	chicken	pot-roasted chicken with mushrooms

2 a cooking of prepared foods in liquid at boiling point
water, milk, stock, court-bouillon

   b e.g. boiled turbot hollandaise sauce
boiled silverside, dumplings and carrots
cream of chicken soup
Vichy carrots   *pp24–25 PC*

   c i old, tough, cheap cuts are rendered palatable, fuel economy,
suitable large scale cookery, nutritious; labour saving

      ii cooking time 20 minutes per lb plus 20 minutes over

   d correct size containers; movement of pans on stove; position
of pan handles; adding or removing foods from containers of
boiling liquids   *pp24–25 PC*

3 a cooking of foods in liquid below boiling point;
easy to digest, tender texture, makes food safe to eat and
pleasant to taste   *p26 PC*

   b shallow; e.g. fillets of sole Duglèré
deep; e.g. poached eggs on spinach with cheese sauce

   c cutting food in even pieces tying to retain shape; making
neater and smaller; drying off cooking liquor from food before
coating with sauce; straining off cooking liquor and reducing
quantity by rapid boiling

   d control of temperature to ensure cooking liquor does not fall
below correct degree; control of time ensures food properly
cooked   *p26 PC*

4 a slow cooking of food in pieces in minimum liquid on top of
stove or in oven; economic and nutritional, makes cheaper
cuts suitable   *pp26–28 PC*

   b combination of unpassed ingredients; thickening cooking
liquor; cooking in the sauce   *pp26–28 PC*

   c during slow process connective tissue converted to gelatine;
protein coagulated but not toughened; lower cooking
temperature   *pp26–28 PC*

    d e.g. Irish stew; chicken curry; ratatouille

5 **a** meat juices retained; little evaporation; nutrients conserved; tenderises; economical   *pp26–28 PC*

    b suitable size pans; care; removal of lids; warning on hot pans; pan handles   *pp26–28 PC*

    c wash hot detergent water; rinse hot water; dry; grease moving parts; correct pan storage; check loose handles; tin linings on copper pans   *pp26–28 PC*

    d saucepans; boiling pans; bratt pans; ovenproof dishes

6 **a** cooking in liquid in covered pan in the oven gives variety, tenderises, and makes food digestible, palatable   *p28 PC*

    b brown – sealed, browned, flavourings added, oven cooked; e.g. beef olives
white – blanched, refreshed, cooked in white stock; e.g. braised celery

    c breakdown of tissue fibre, softens texture, tenderises, less expensive meats can be used, retention of nutrients, variety on menu   *p28 PC*

    d applying heat to meat surface; inserting fat in strips; steeping in pickling liquid; extracting flavour   *p28 PC*

7 **a** cooking of prepared foods by moist heat; to make food digestible, of edible texture, safe, nutritious   *pp29–30 PC*

    b low pressure; high pressure; between plates over a pan of boiling water   *pp29–30 PC*

    c change in structure and texture; retention of nutrients, digestible, speed, labour-saving; batch cooking, economical   *pp29–30 PC*

    d e.g. steamed halibut, shrimp sauce; steak and kidney pudding; steamed potatoes; orange sponge pudding

8 **a** food cooked in vacuum sealed plastic pouches by steam; minimal changes in texture/reduced weight loss, labour saving; no drying out/colour loss; food cooks in own juices   *p29 PC*

    b check water levels if applicable; ball arm moves freely; reduce steam pressure before opening door to reduce risk of scalds   *p29 PC*

    c **i**   placing of food in prepared moulds;
       ii   filling of steamer trays with moulds;
      iii placing trays in steamer;
      iv moulds clean and lightly greased   *p29 PC*

9   **a**   cooking of food by dry heat in an oven; make food digestible, palatable, safe; eye appeal; variety of textures; popularity
pp30–31 PC

    b   dry baking plus steam from food; increased humidity/addition of water or steam in oven; bain-marie/heat modification
pp30–31 PC

    c   variety; eye appeal; aromas; uniformity of bulk cooking; ovens with effective temperature controls; easy access for loading/removal
pp30–31 PC

    d   **i** cutting with sharp blade;   **ii** egg, sugar or milk brushed on before or after cooking;   **iii** use of wire grids/air circulation; **iv** presentation improvements;   **v** time required for oven temperature to return to correct degree before continuing cooking;   **vi** light sprinkling of flour, or icing or castor sugar
pp30–31 PC

10   **a**   cooking in dry heat with fat in oven, or on spit, to cook food until tender, digestible, safe, palatable   *p32 PC*

    b   surface protein of meat sealed to help retain natural juices and keep meat succulent – juices for gravy; controlled energy use and temperature; minimal fire risk   *p32 PC*

    c   ovens pre-heated; oven temperatures in recipes followed; cooking time affected by shape, size, type, bone formation and quality meat thermometers   *p32 PC*

    d   suitable sized trays; careful handling; suitable dry cloths; food securely held before removal from tray   *p32 PC*

11   **a**   quick cooking by radiant heat; over heat – on preheated greased bars; under heat – salamander; between heat – between grill bars or plates; speed of cooking – maximum retention of nutrients   *pp33–35 PC*

    b   rare – red and bloody
underdone – reddish pink
just done – pink
well done – clean   *pp33–35 PC*

    c   e.g. grilled herring with mustard sauce; mixed grill; grilled tomatoes; Welsh rarebit

    d   seal and colour on hot grill; basting – use of tongs, palette knives; care when moving hot salamander and grill bars; use edged trays; care when removing foods

12   **a**   cooking food in small quantity of fat in shallow pan or flat surface;   *pp35–37 PC*
shallow fry – meunière – presentation side first
sauté – tender meat in sauté or frying pan – deglazing

griddle – solid metal plate

stir fry – fast cooking in wok or frying pan   *pp35–37 PC*

b   instant coagulation of protein retaining juices; change in
nutritional content; quick rapid cooking   *pp35–37 PC*

Menu examples

> fried eggs and bacon
> shallow fried plaice fillets with
> cucumber
> shallow fried sirloin steak with
> red wine sauce
> breadcrumbed breast of chicken
> with asparagus
> shallow fried Belgian endive
> shallow fried banana flamed with
> rum

c   e.g. omelet pan; bratt pan   *pp35–37 PC*

d   correct pan size; sleeves rolled down; care when placing food
in hot fat; thick, clean, dry cloths for cleaning; move loaded
hot pans carefully on stove

13   a   cooking of food in deep fat or oil; coat with milk and flour –
batter – egg and crumb etc.; blanching – partial deep frying
                pp37–39 PC

b   surface sealed, minimum absorption of fat on coated items;
uncoated items absorb more fat; partial cooking or blanching
helps busy service; wide variety of foods possible; coated food
quickly sealed; fast cooking; easy handling   *pp37–39 PC*

c   systematic working; no overfilling; never allow fat to overheat;
no excess of food in fryer; allow recovery time; reduce
temperatures as business slackens – restrict holding time; strain
fat daily; cover fat when not in use; half fill fryers; no
overloading; dry food; place food in fat carefully; basket and
spider to hand; fire equipment; sleeves down; thick, dry, clean
cloths for handling   *pp37–39 PC*

d   e.g. Scotch eggs and salad; fish cakes, tomato sauce; croquette
potatoes; French fried onions; doughnuts

14   a   high frequency power; electricity agitation of water molecules
in food causing heat/friction; cooks raw food; re-heats cooked
food; defrosts frozen food   *pp39–42 PC*

b time saving; fast; economical on energy and labour; meals available 24 hours a day; food cooks in own juices; minimal shrinkage and drying-out; flexibility;
not suitable for all foods; limited cooking space; penetration depth of microwaves limited   *p107 PC*

c correct selection of cooking/time controls; certain foods e.g. fish – remove when underdone to finish cooking; use suitable containers e.g. glass, china etc.; cook even-shaped items; keep food level i.e. not mounds; sufficient space for storing; cover most foods   *p107 PC*

d coloration; cannot use metal pans   *p108 PC*

15 a danger to food – chemical e.g. copper
                         plant e.g. toadstools
                         micro-organisms e.g. bacteria   *pp7–14 PC*
food poisoning sources; spreading methods; growth factors; potentially dangerous foods e.g. made-up meat dishes; preventions – care of person, of food, of environment

b adequate mise-en-place; work flow; food kept cool; garnish and decorate close to service time   *pp84–85 PC*

c appearance clean and fresh, appealing to the eye, appetite stimulating, nutritional value

d e.g. chicken and ham pie; orange bavarois

STOCKS, SOUPS AND SAUCES

CHAPTER 4

Read pp 43–81 of *Practical Cookery.*

Stocks and sauces

SHORT QUESTIONS

1   Explain what is understood by the term 'stock' when it relates to a liquid used in the kitchen.

2   Why is beef stock cooked for a longer time than fish stock?

3   Why does stock go cloudy?
    boiled insufficiently; boiled for too long; boiled too slowly; boiled too quickly

4   State four points which indicate a good stock.

5   To achieve good quality stock it is necessary to . . .

6   After rapid cooling, below what temperature should stock be refrigerated?

7   If stock is to be deep frozen, how should it be stored?

8   Describe the procedure for using frozen stock.

9   Why should liquids never be stored above eye level?

10   Why is salt omitted from stock?
    it prevents it from simmering; it causes it to go sour; it makes it change colour; stock is used as a base for many dishes

11   Why is it necessary to skim stock?

12   What is the purpose of having brown and white beef stock in the kitchen?

13   What are the proportions of ingredients needed for stock (other than fish stock)?

14   Describe the difference between producing a brown stock and a white stock.

15   Why is the time taken to cook fish stock important?

16   What are fish glaze and meat glaze?

17   Why are fish glaze and meat glaze used?
        increase flavour; save money and time; improve the appearance; improve texture

18   A sauce is a thickened liquid; name four ways in which the liquid can be thickened.

19   State four points which indicate a good quality sauce.

20   What is a roux?
        a thickening; a type of saucepan; an unusual vegetable; a Russian sweet

21   Name three roux and three stocks and give an example of a suitable sauce for each.

22   Why should a boiling liquid never be added to a hot roux?

23   Name three ingredients which may be used to thicken jus lié.

24   What is understood by the word 'dilute'?
        to add liquid; to drain in a colander; to pass through a sieve; to put in a bain-marie

25   How many portions will four litres of white onion sauce produce?

26   What two main items are needed to produce a velouté?

27   Name four velouté sauces.

28   What two items may be used to finish a velouté sauce?

29   What is caper sauce traditionally served with?
        boiled mutton; boiled bacon; boiled beef; boiled fish

30   A . . . sauce is used in chicken vol-au-vent.

31   Name three sauces which are derivatives of a velouté.

32   Name six sauces which are derived from jus lié or well reduced stock.

33 What is the name of the sauce which contains chopped shallots, sliced mushrooms, tomatoes, chopped parsley and tarragon?

34 What may devilled sauce be served with?
   grilled meat; cold meat; roast meat; boiled meat

35 What is the main ingredient in sauce lyonnaise:
   mushrooms; shallots; gherkins; onions

36 With what dish may sauce lyonnaise be served?

37 What are chopped capers and chopped gherkins used in?
   sauce Robert; sauce poivrade; sauce piquante; or sauce charcutière

38 Describe sauce Reform.

39 Name a well-known dish in which sauce Reform is used.

40 What points indicate a high standard of roast gravy?

41 Name two dishes with which bread sauce is traditionally served.

42 Why is apple sauce served with roast pork, duck and goose?

43 Cranberry sauce is served with roast turkey: true/false.

44 Match the following sauces with an appropriate dish.
   a bread   fried lamb cutlets
   b mint   roast chicken
   c tomato   fried liver
   d lyonnaise   roast lamb
   e curry   fried fish
   f Reform   hard boiled eggs

45 Name two different dishes with which hollandaise sauce may be served.

46 Why may hollandaise sauce curdle?

47 How can the curdling of hollandaise sauce be avoided?

48 How can curdled hollandaise sauce be rectified?
   by adding butter; by whisking in a little hot water; by increasing the temperature; by more whisking

49 When handling warm egg-based sauces, what two factors can assist in the prevention of *salmonella* infection?

50 Why is a compound butter sauce served with grilled fish?

51   Give four reasons why mayonnaise may curdle.

52   Name two sauces which are thickened by using eggs.

53   Which ingredients are needed to produce tartar sauce from mayonnaise sauce?

54   With what dish is horseradish sauce served?
       roast beef; roast lamb; roast veal; roast venison

55   Mint sauce is traditionally served with . . . ?

56   Why is it very important to observe hygienic standards when using aspic jelly and chaudfroid sauce?

57   What points of quality would indicate a high standard aspic jelly?

58   Sauces such as tomato, béchamel etc. form a skin on the surface; suggest how this can be prevented.

QUESTIONS IN DEPTH

1   **a**   Give the principles for making good stock.
       b   What are the differences between making white meat, brown meat, fish, and vegetable stocks?
       c   Describe a glaze, the method of making and its use.
       d   Give the definition of a sauce, four ways in which a sauce can be thickened and two menu examples from each method.

2   **a**   What is a roux, what are the three degrees to which it may be cooked and what safety precaution should be observed when adding liquid to a roux?
       b   Name three fats or oils that can be used for making a roux.
       c   What is meant by dextrinisation and what can be its effect in a roux?
       d   Name the basic sauce and two derivations that can be made from white, blond and brown roux.

3   **a**   Give the proportion of ingredients and method of making:
       i roast gravy;   **ii** jus lié;   **iii** bread sauce;   **iv** apple sauce;
       and suggest a suitable dish with which each could be served.
       b   Give method of making horseradish, mint, and Cumberland sauces; and suggest a suitable dish with which each could be served.
       c   Name three compound butter sauces, give the ingredients for each and a suitable dish with which each could be served.

4 a Explain the method of making hollandaise sauce and state the proportion of ingredients required.

   b Give reasons why it may curdle and the remedy.

   c What essential points regarding food safety and hygiene must be observed when making and keeping the sauce warm?

   d Give three menu examples of the use of this sauce and describe and name a related sauce with a menu example.

SHORT QUESTIONS – **ANSWERS** _____

1 a liquid containing some of the soluble nutrients and flavours of food which are extracted by gentle simmering   *p45 PC*

2 because 20 minutes is sufficient to extract the flavour from fish bones whereas 6–8 hours are required for beef bones

3 boiled too quickly

4 flavour; colour; clarity; non-greasy

5 use sound ingredients; bring to the boil, skim then simmer; skim frequently; do not over or under cook

6 below 5°C (42°F)

7 stored below –18°C (0°F) and labelled and dated

8 stock must be boiled for at least two minutes and not reheated more than once

9 possibility of contents spilling over a person unable to see them

10 stock is used as a base for many dishes; if the stock were salted, as it reduced in cooking the end product could be over-salted

11 to remove grease and scum and retain the quality of the stock

12 white stock for white stews, sauces, soups etc.; brown stock for brown stews, sauces, soups etc.

13 2kg (4lb) bones; 4½ litres (1 gallon) water; 400g (1lb) vegetables
                                                                     p46 PC

14 for a brown stock the bones and vegetables are coloured. For white stock bones and vegetables are used raw

15 overcooking spoils flavour

16 fish and meat stock steadily reduced to a sticky consistency

p48 PC

17 increase flavour

18 roux; egg yolks; cornflour etc.; beurre manié   *pp49–50 PC*

19 smooth; glossy appearance; definite taste; light texture

20 a thickening

21 white roux – milk – Béchamel; blond roux – stock – velouté;
    brown roux – stock – demi-glace

22 because heavy steam will result which could cause a burn or
    scald

23 cornflour; arrowroot; potato flour

24 to add liquid

25 60–80 portions

26 blond roux; stock

27 caper; suprême; mushroom; ivory

28 egg yolks and cream

29 boiled mutton

30 velouté

31 aurore; ivory; mushroom

32 Red wine; chasseur; devil; pepper; Italian; Madeira

33 chasseur

34 grilled meat

35 onions

36 e.g. Vienna steaks

37 sauce piquante

38 a well flavoured or reduced stock or jus lié with the addition of
    red-currant jelly and a garnish of julienne of beetroot, egg white,
    gherkin, mushroom, truffle, tongue

39 Lamb cutlets Reform

40   appetising brown colour; not greasy; good flavour

41   roast chicken; roast pheasant

42   because the sharpness of the apple sauce complements the richness of the flesh and aids digestion

43   true

44   **a**   roast chicken
         b   roast lamb
         c   fried fish
         d   fried liver
         e   hard boiled eggs
         f   fried lamb cutlets

45   e.g. poached salmon; trout; broccoli

46   too fierce heat; butter added too quickly

47   whisk egg yolks over gentle heat, allow to cool slightly, add butter slowly   *p63 PC*

48   by whisking in a little hot water

49   use pasteurised egg yolks; discard after keeping warm for two hours

50   because if thick slices are placed on the fish just prior to the fish being served, it will just begin to melt and be soft for the customer to use

51   oil added quickly; oil too cold; insufficient whisking; stale egg yolks   *p88 PC*

52   mayonnaise; hollandaise

53   gherkins; capers; parsley   *p89 PC*

54   roast beef

55   roast lamb

56   because they both contain gelatine, a meat based product*, and are likely to become contaminated if not kept and used under refrigeration (*a suitable medium for bacterial growth)
                                                                           pp90–91 PC

57   crystal clarity; appetising colour; good flavour   *pp90–91 PC*

58   add a thin layer of butter on top of the sauces

QUESTIONS IN DEPTH – **OUTLINE ANSWERS** _____

1   a   foundation of many preparations; maximum care necessary; use sound ingredients; remove scum; degrease; simmer; maintain temperature; no salt; refrigerate if kept   *pp46–47 PC*

    b   white stock – bones blanched
brown stock – bones and vegetables browned
fish stock – 20 minutes cooking only
vegetable stock – 1 hour cooking only

    c   reduced stock; reduce stock to gelatinous consistency; used for flavour strengthening or improving

    d   lightly thickened liquid; roux, beurre manié, arrowroot, egg yolks; e.g. béchamel, moules marinières, jus lié, hollandaise

2   a   combination fat and flour
white; blond; brown
never add boiling liquid to hot roux   *pp50–53 PC*

    b   butter; margarine; vegetable oil; dripping

    c   chemical change in flour; sauce may become thin because the starch is broken down and loses its thickening property

    d   béchamel e.g. mornay sauce; velouté e.g. caper sauce; espagnole e.g. chasseur sauce

3   a   i   roast gravy for roast meats e.g. roast leg of lamb – 250ml (1pt) stock, 200g (8oz) bones, 125g (5oz) vegetables all browned and simmered for 2 hours

        ii   jus lié for pot roasted meat or chicken – 200g (8oz) meat to 500ml (1pt) stock and 10g (½oz) arrowroot/cornflour; well flavoured brown stock simmered for 15 minutes with diluted arrowroot or cornflour

        iii   bread sauce with roast game/chicken – 375ml (¾pt) milk flavoured with studded onion, thickened with breadcrumbs

        iv   apple sauce with roast pork – 400g (1lb) apples, 25g (1oz) sugar, 25g (1oz) butter cooked to purée

    b   combine grated horseradish, vinegar, cream – roast beef;
combine chopped mint, vinegar, sugar – roast lamb;
combine redcurrant jelly, chopped shallots, port, lemon, orange, mustard – cold ham

    c   parsley – 300g (12oz) butter, parsley, lemon juice – grilled steak

anchovy – butter and anchovy essence – grilled sole
shrimp – 50g (2oz) butter, 50g (2oz) shrimps – grilled plaice

4 a   reduction (optional) yolks cooked to a sabayon, melted butter
whisked in – 2 yolks, 200g (8oz) butter   *p63 PC*

b   excess heat – butter added too quickly
use a teaspoon of boiling water and/or another yolk and
slowly whisk on the curdled mixture

c   pan, whisk and strainer perfectly clean, butter fresh; sauce kept
in clean receptacle for service; use pasteurised yolks, do not
keep sauce warm longer than two hours, then discard

d   boiled or steamed turbot, asparagus, cauliflower
béarnaise – grilled steak

Soups

SHORT QUESTIONS

1   Classify the soups.

2   Give an example for each class of soup.

3   How much soup is usually served per portion?
125ml (5fl oz); 250ml (10fl oz); 375ml (15fl oz); 500ml
(20fl oz)

4   Suggest two ways of making a cream soup.

5   Specify the points which indicate a high standard consommé.

6   State the factors needed to produce a good quality consommé.

7   What should the colour of consommé be?
brown; amber; pale amber; dark brown

8   Suggest six garnishes suitable for adding to consommé and state
how each should be written on the menu.

9   What have consommé en tasse and consommé madrilène in
common?

10   Which stock is used to produce Scotch broth?
mutton; beef; fish; chicken

11   Name the cereal used to garnish Scotch broth.

12 What characteristics has a broth of good quality?

13 What is a soup thickened by its main ingredient called?
        velouté; purée; broth; potage

14 Which class of soup is accompanied by croûtons?

15 Describe the points which indicate good quality croûtons.

16 What are lentils, yellow split peas, harricot beans and green split peas?

17 How is a good standard achieved when making a purée soup?

18 What is a flute?
        diced fried bread; a roll; long thin loaf; a cheese straw

19 Minestrone originates from where?
        Spain; Portugal; France; Italy

20 What are the accompaniments to minestrone?

QUESTIONS IN DEPTH

1   a   Classify the different types of soup and give two examples for each.
    b   Specify the ingredients and method of making consommé.
    c   Explain the cause of the clarification process and give six reasons why consommé can go cloudy.
    d   Give ingredients and method for making a royale.

2   a   Describe the quality of a finished velouté, purée and consommé soup.
    b   Name four pulse soups, four vegetable soups and explain how they may be garnished.
    c   State four variations for a basic tomato soup.
    d   Suggest six different soups using interesting combinations of two or more vegetables in each. Describe how they may be finished and garnished.

SHORT QUESTIONS – ANSWERS

1   clear broth; purée, velouté; cream; bisque; miscellaneous   *p65 PC*

2   e.g. clear, Scotch broth   *p65 PC*

3   250ml (10fl oz)

4   a purée finished with cream or/and milk
     a purée using half stock, half béchamel   *p69 PC*

5   crystal clear; no grease or fat; good flavour

6   good fresh ingredients; good quality stock; careful method of
     clarification; care when straining   *p66 PC*

7   amber

8   e.g. Royal clear soup; Consommé brunoise   *p67 PC*

9   they are both served chilled

10   mutton

11   barley   *p68 PC*

12   well flavoured stock and plenty of vegetables

13   purée   *p69 PC*

14   purée   *p69 PC*

15   neatly and evenly cut; golden brown colour; crisp and good flavour

16   pulses   *p68 PC*

17   sound fresh ingredients; careful preparation and cooking; not
     overcooking; light consistency; good seasoning

18   long thin loaf

19   Italy

20   grated parmesan cheese; thinly sliced toasted flutes

QUESTIONS IN DEPTH – OUTLINE ANSWERS _____

1   a   cream; purée; broth; consommé; bisque; velouté;
         miscellaneous   *pp65–81 PC*
         e.g. cream of mushroom; potato soup, Scotch broth;
         consommé royale; minestrone
     b   beef, vegetables, egg whites, stock, seasoning – mix the
         minced beef, vegetables, egg whites and stock, bring slowly to
         the boil, simmer for two hours, strain
     c   coagulation of egg albumen and meat absorbing all other
         ingredients as it rises to the top of the liquid
         e.g. greasy; poor quality stock; imperfect coagulation of the
         clearing agent

d egg, stock or milk, seasoning; whisked egg, liquid and seasoning
   cooked au bain-marie in dariole moulds   *pp65–81 PC*

2 **a** velouté – velvet smooth consistency, not too thick, seasoned
   lightly, well flavoured
   purée – smooth, well flavoured with main ingredients,
   seasoned, pleasing colour
   consommé – crystal clear, amber colour, good flavour, lightly
   seasoned

   b e.g. lentil; green pea; yellow split pea; haricot bean – served
   with croutons
   e.g. carrot; watercress; celery; cauliflower – garnish with small
   diced carrot, watercress leaves, small diced celery, very small
   florets of cauliflower

   c e.g. ½ potato, ½ tomato; finished with cream; orange
   flavoured; finished with basil

   d e.g. celeriac and potato; leek and potato; mixed root
   vegetables; Jerusalem artichoke and potato; tomato and
   mushroom; asparagus and leek
   Finished with cream, yoghurt, creme fraiche, milk, diced
   vegetables, blanched leaves, herbs, flavours e.g. orange, lemon

HORS-D'OEUVRE, SALADS COOKED/CURED/PREPARED FOODS

CHAPTER 5

Read pp 82–117 of *Practical Cookery*.

SHORT QUESTIONS

1   What do you understand by the term 'hors-d'oeuvre'?

2   Into what three main categories may hors-d'oeuvre be divided?

3   What accompaniments are served with oysters?
      brown bread and butter and lemon; white bread and butter
      and lemon; melba toast and lemon; toast and lemon

4   From which fish is caviar obtained?
      shad; salmon trout; sturgeon; salmon

5   What part of the fish is caviar?
      the roe; the marrow; the young fish; the brain

6   How should oysters be served?
      in a coupe; on a canapé; on a julienne of lettuce;
      on crushed ice

7   How many oysters are usually served as a portion?
      four; five; six; eight

8   What is pâté usually cooked in?
      timbale; sauteuse; terrine; ravier

9   For grapefruit cocktail the grapefruit is cut into:
      halves; quarters; segments; dice

10 State the points which indicate a well prepared grapefruit cocktail.

11 What have the following in common?
      ogen, charentais, honeydew, cantaloup

12   Suggest three ways of serving avocado pear.

13   The basic sauce for a shellfish cocktail is:
        mayonnaise; béchamel; hollandaise; fish velouté

14   What is the culinary meaning of 'soused'?
        pickled in alcohol; kippered in smoke; cooked in vinegar;
        saturated in oil

15   Name two kinds of fish which may be soused.

16   Suggest two ways of presenting a variety of hors-d'oeuvre.

17   Egg mayonnaise is presented in three ways on the menu; describe
     each, stating how much egg per portion would be used.

18   Suggest four points to be considered when preparing a selection
     of hors-d'oeuvre.

19   Compile a list of eight items that can be included in a selection of
     hors-d'oeuvre.

20   Name five items which could be prepared à la grecque.

21   If a dish is termed Portuguese-style which ingredient will be
     included?
        tunny; cucumber; sweetcorn; tomato

22   Give four reasons for the popularity of cold foods.

23   What is essential to making cold foods appeal to the customer?

24   Explain the importance of temperature and hygiene.

25   Why is personal hygiene particularly important?

26   What is the purpose of having cold preparations?

27   Why are foods taken from the refrigerator allowed to stand at
     room temperature for 5–10 minutes?

28   How may the risk of contamination be reduced when preparing
     cold foods?

29   List the main ingredients for fish cooking liquid.

30   Suggest three ways of serving cold salmon and describe their
     presentation.

31   Explain the preparation of salmon prior to cooking.

32   When cooked, why is the salmon left in the cooking liquid?

33 Suggest six cold meat or poultry items.

34 Describe how cold meats may be served.

35 Name two hams which are eaten raw.

36 Name two English hams.

37 What are the main considerations when using pâtés and terrines?

38 Explain the difference between chicken salad and chicken mayonnaise.

39 What is hot water paste used for?

40 Name two dishes using hot water paste.

41 What is the difference between a simple salad and a composed salad?

42 What ingredients could you serve in a bowl of mixed salad?

43 What are the usual ingredients in a French salad?

44 What does a Florida salad consist of?
　　　lettuce and grapes; lettuce and grapefruit; lettuce and orange; lettuce and tomato

45 What dressing would you offer with a Florida salad?

46 The chief ingredients of a salad niçoise are:
　　　French beans, anchovies, potatoes, capers, olives, tomatoes;
　　　French beans, peas, carrots, turnips, anchovies, olives;
　　　French beans, tomatoes, potatoes, anchovies, olives, turnips;
　　　French beans, lettuce, onions, pimentos, anchovies, olives

47 Name three dressings.

48 Why may mayonnaise curdle?

49 How may mayonnaise be thinned?

50 What ingredients may be added to vary mayonnaise?

51 With what may green sauce be served?

52 What additions to mayonnaise are needed to make tartare sauce?

53 With what are horseradish and mint sauces served?

54 A dressing should always be offered with a salad: true/false.

55 What are the four chief ingredients added to vinaigrette to make thousand island dressing?

56   What is added to cream to make an acidulated cream dressing?

57   Name four suitable ingredients that may be added to vinaigrette in order to give variation.

QUESTIONS IN DEPTH

1   **a**   Name the three categories into which hors-d'oeuvre can be divided. Give an example for each and describe the ingredients and method for preparing each item.

   b   Give ingredients and method for a basic vinaigrette and suggest further ingredients that can be used for variation.

   c   Give the balance of ingredients and method of making mayonnaise. Suggest two derivations and name two menu items for each.

   d   Give the reasons why a mayonnaise may turn or curdle and how it can be rethickened.

2   **a**   Name and give ingredients for two compound salads from a vegetable base and two from a fruit base.

   b   State three ways by which cross contamination between cooked and uncooked food can be prevented.

   c   How are avocado pears tested for ripeness? Name and give ingredients for three ways of serving avocado pears and describe how the avocado is peeled, sliced and fanned.

3   **a**   Briefly describe eight interesting varieties of hors-d'oeuvre.

   b   List the ingredients and method of preparing coleslaw and celeriac salad.

   c   Give the ingredients and method for hors-d'oeuvre à la grecque and indicate four items that can be prepared by this method.

   d   **i**   What ingredients would be served for a green salad?
      ii   What ingredients for a mixed salad?
      iii   What dressing can be offered?

SHORT QUESTIONS — ANSWERS _____

1   appetising first course dishes

2   single food items; selection of dishes; well seasoned hot dishes
p86 PC

3   brown bread and butter and lemon   *p91 PC*

4   sturgeon   *p91 PC*

5   the roe   *p91 PC*

6   on crushed ice   *p91 PC*

7   six   *p91 PC*

8   terrine   *p93 PC*

9   segments   *p93 PC*

10 neatly cut segments, no pips, no white pith

11 types of melon   *p97 PC*

12 e.g. with vinaigrette; crabmeat; prawns

13 mayonnaise   *p98 PC*

14 cooked in vinegar   *p99 PC*

15 herring; mackerel   *p99 PC*

16 ready served on a plate – in raviers

17 as part of a selection of hors-d'oeuvre – eggs quartered, halved or
    sliced lightly coated with mayonnaise;
    as an individual hors-d'oeuvre (one egg);   *p101 PC*
    as a main course (two eggs)

18 e.g. variety of choice; colour; ingredients; seasonings

19 e.g. egg mayonnaise; salami; sardines; vegetable salad; meat salad;
    fish salad; tomato; rice salad

20 cauliflower; artichokes; button onions; leeks; celery   *p109 PC*

21 tomato   *p110 PC*

22 visual appeal; can be self service; prepared in advance; large
    numbers quickly served

23 must appear fresh; look attractive; decorated but not over
    garnished; variety of texture

24 dishes prepared in advance must be kept refrigerated. Where
    possible keep in refrigerated cabinets for display or screened, cover
    with cling film

25 foods will go direct to consumer: no further cooking or heating
    which would kill bacteria, therefore hand washing and wearing
    plastic gloves is vital when handling cold foods

26 add variety to menu and foods suitable in hot weather; provide raw foods enhancing nutritional value; stimulate appetite if presented attractively

27 so that they are served at their best regarding flavour

28 before, during and after assembly keep in a cold place, refrigerator or cold room to reduce risk

29 water; carrots; onion; herbs; vinegar

30 whole salmon; mayonnaise; salmon salad   *pp111–113 PC*

whole – decorated or garnished
mayonnaise – flaked, coated, with mayonnaise and decorated
salad – not coated
p190 PC

31 remove scales and gills, intestines and blood from backbone, trim off fins and wash well   *p113 PC*

32 to keep moist   *p113 PC*

33 e.g. roast turkey, chicken, beef, pork, ham, tongue   *p115 PC*

34 in joints with small amount carved; carved in slices; jointed poultry

35 e.g. Parma, Bayonne, Ardennes

36 e.g. York, Bradenham

37 to be kept refrigerated as much as possible

38 chicken salad – the mayonnaise is separate; chicken mayonnaise is coated with the sauce

39 cold pies

40 e.g. raised pork pie; veal and ham pie   *p116 PC*

41 simple salad – individual item e.g. lettuce or tomato; composed salad – combination of ingredients

42 lettuce, tomato, watercress etc.

43 lettuce, tomato, cucumber

44 lettuce and grapefruit

45 sour cream

46 French beans, anchovies, potatoes, capers, olives, tomatoes

47 e.g. vinaigrette; roquefort; thousand island

48 oil added too quickly; oil too cold; insufficiently whisked; stale yolk   *p88 PC*

49 with water or vinegar   *p88 PC*

50 e.g. herbs; garlic juice; cheese; tomato; peppers

51 cold salmon or salmon trout

52 chopped capers, gherkins and parsley

53 horseradish – beef roast; mint – roast lamb

54 true

55 pimento; egg; parsley and tomato ketchup

56 lemon juice

57 e.g. English or French mustard; chopped herbs

QUESTIONS IN DEPTH – OUTLINE ANSWERS

1 **a** **i** Single cold food item e.g. smoked salmon, pâté, grapefruit; e.g. halve the grapefruit, cut between segments serve with a maraschino cherry in centre in a coupe *p84 PC*

ii a selection of cold dishes e.g. potato, meat, fish salads, tomato, beetroot, sardine etc.; e.g. cooked sliced potatoes, chopped chive vinaigrette bound with mayonnaise
pp100–109 PC

iii hot dishes e.g. mushrooms, bouchées, mushrooms Portuguese-style – chopped onion, oil tomatoes, garlic seasoning, mushrooms cooked together and served hot
p88 PC

b 3–6 parts oil to 1 part vinegar, mustard, salt, pepper; English/continental mustard, herbs, chopped egg, lemon juice

c ½pt oil, 2 yolks, seasoning, 2tsps vinegar
whisk yolks, vinegar, seasoning. Slowly mix in oil, finish with boiling water
tartare sauce – fried plaice fillets; green sauce – cold salmon

d oil added quickly; oil too cold; insufficient whisking; stale yolks
boiling water in clean bowl, slowly whisk in curdled sauce or fresh yolk; with little water – whisk in curdled sauce

2   a   e.g. vegetable salad – carrots, turnips, peas, beans, vinaigrette, mayonnaise
Waldorf salad – apple, celery, walnuts, mayonnaise, lettuce

    b   use separate chopping boards for different foods e.g. meat, fish; wash hands between handling raw and cooked foods; separate storage for raw and cooked food

    c   base should give under gentle thumb pressure
e.g. with shrimps bound with mayonnaise; with crabmeat bound with shellfish cocktail sauce
cut in half lengthwise, remove stone, peel off skin, slice lengthwise on to serving dish and fan-out

3   a   e.g. hard boiled eggs, mayonnaise
potato salad – sliced cooked potatoes, chives, vinaigrette, mayonnaise
meat salad – cooked meat, gherkins, French beans, tomatoes, vinaigrette, sliced tomato and cucumber
three bean salad – three pulses, herbs, chives, vinaigrette
fish salad – cooked fish, hard boiled egg, herbs, lettuce vinaigrette

    b   finely shredded cabbage, carrot, natural yoghurt or mayonnaise; fine julienne celeriac, lemon, mustard, mayonnaise or yoghurt

    c   oil, lemon juice, herbs cooked with named vegetable e.g. artichokes, button onions, cauliflower, celery

    d   e.g. i   lettuce (assorted)
          ii   lettuce; tomato; cucumber; watercress
          iii vinaigrette in both cases

EGGS

CHAPTER 6

Read pp 197–212 of *Practical Cookery.*

SHORT QUESTIONS

1   Describe what happens if scrambled eggs are overcooked.

2   When cooking scrambled eggs what points need particular attention?

3   When cooking scrambled eggs in bulk what precaution can be taken to reduce the risk of *salmonella* infection.

4   How long does it take to cook egg in cocotte?
     1–2 minutes; 2–3 minutes; 3–4 minutes; 4–5 minutes

5   Suggest two suitable garnishes for egg in cocotte.

6   Match the appropriate cooking method of eggs to the approximate cooking time.
     a   hard-boiled eggs   3–5 minutes
     b   soft-boiled eggs   8–10 minutes
     c   boiled egg   5½ minutes

7   Suggest two ways of using hard-boiled eggs.

8   Explain how Scotch eggs may be served hot and cold.

9   At which meal is a boiled egg normally served?
     breakfast; lunch; dinner; supper

10   Describe a properly cooked poached egg.

11   Why is a little vinegar added to water when poaching eggs?

12   What is the price of eggs?

13   Why is it essential to use fresh eggs for poaching?

14   List the eggs used for culinary purposes.

15   How are eggs graded?

16   State the quality points for eggs.

17   What is the food value of eggs?

18   How may the risk of salmonella food poisoning caused by eggs be reduced?

19   How should eggs be stored?

20   Why may eggs be described as 'versatile'?

OMELETS

21   List five points which must be observed to produce a good omelet.

22   Name three flat omelets.

23   What is the garnish for the omelets named in the previous question?

QUESTIONS IN DEPTH

1   a   When using beaten eggs in large quantities, e.g. omelets and scrambled eggs, what procedure can be used to reduce risk of salmonella poisoning?
    b   What causes dark rings forming around the yolks of hard boiled eggs?

2   a   Suggest six different methods of cooking eggs, and give two menu examples for each method.
    b   Explain the making of scrambled eggs and explain the effects of over-cooking.
    c   Outline the method for producing poached eggs.
    d   State the method for making omelets, describe the three basic types and give a menu example for each.

SHORT QUESTIONS – ANSWERS

1   protein toughens; eggs discolour; syneresis (water separation) occurs   *p120 PC*

2   slow cooking; constant stirring; remove from heat before cooking is completed   *p120 PC*

3   use pasteurised eggs

4   2–3 minutes   *p121 PC*

5   e.g. creamed minced chicken, tomato concassée   *p121 PC*

6   a 8–10 minutes;   b 5½ minutes;   c 3–5 minutes

7   e.g. hard boiled eggs with mushroom and cheese sauce   *p122 PC*
        hard boiled eggs with cheese and tomato sauce

8   hot with tomato sauce; cold with salad   *p124 PC*

9   breakfast

10 firm tender white, slightly thickened unbroken yolk   *p123 PC*

11 to assist in setting the egg white and prevent it spreading *p123 PC*

12 current market price

13 the white of stale or poor quality eggs will spread too thinly
                                                                p123 PC

14 Hens, ducks, turkey, geese, guinea fowl, quail, gulls   *p119 PC*

15 Small, medium, large, extra large

16 clean; high proportion of thick to thin white; rounded firm yolk

17 eggs contain most of the nutrients; are low in calories; easily
    digested; a protective food, provides energy and material for
    growth and repair

18 using pasteurised where appropriate

19 cool place, preferably refrigerated; away from strong smelling
    foods; first in first out

20 they can be used for a very wide variety of dishes for lunch, high
    teas, supper, snacks and many breakfast dishes; they are also used
    for thickening, enriching, colouring, binding

21 e.g. clean hot pan; good fresh fat; lightly seasoned well beaten
    eggs; rapid cooking; not overcooking   *p126 PC*

22 e.g. Spanish   *p126 PC*

23 Spanish – tomato, onion, pimento   *p126 PC*

QUESTIONS IN DEPTH – **OUTLINE ANSWERS** _____

1   a   make use of pasteurised whole eggs and thoroughly cook the
        eggs
    b   high temperature; overcooking; release of iron and sulphur

2   **a**   omelet; boiled; scrambled; en cocotte; sur le plat; poached

Menu examples

> Ham omelet
> Poached eggs with spinach and cheese sauce
> Scrambled eggs with kidneys
> Eggs in a cocotte with creamed chicken
> Eggs on a dish with bacon
> Soft boiled eggs with sweetcorn and cheese sauce

b   beaten eggs lightly cooked in butter over gentle heat stirring continuously
overcooking toughens the protein and eggs discolour by the release of iron and sulphur, syneresis occurs

c   top quality, fresh eggs broken into gently simmering water with a little vinegar

d   beaten, seasoned eggs lightly but swiftly cooked in an omelet pan then carefully shaped
folded – e.g. mushroom
filled – e.g. tomato
flat – e.g. Spanish   *pp119–126 PC*

PASTA AND RICE

CHAPTER 7

Read pp 127–146 of *Practical Cookery*.

SHORT QUESTIONS

1   What do you understand by the term pasta?

2   What is meant by the term 'al dente'?

3   Does fresh egg pasta require more or less cooking time than dried pasta?

4   Name four different flavours that can be incorporated into a pasta dough.

5   What are farinaceous dishes?

6   What is the common term for the majority of farinaceous dishes?

7   Pasta dishes can be offered for any meal or snack: true/false.

8   Why is it necessary to cook pasta in plenty of boiling salted water?

9   Which of the following is usually served separately with pasta dishes?
            croûtons; sippets; cheese; rice

10   What points need particular attention when cooking pasta?

11   Give the names of four pasta dishes.

12   Which of the following is traditionally served with pasta dishes?
            Cheddar; Parmesan; Gruyère; Roquefort

13   What is the sauce used for spaghetti alla pomidoro?

14   What is the garnish for Fettucine Verdi in Salsa cremona?

15   What dusting agent is used when making noodle dough?

16   What is the main ingredient for bolognaise sauce?
            cheese; tomatoes; minced beef; mushrooms

17 Into what shape are noodles cut?

18 Puff paste is used to produce ravioli: true/false.

19 Explain the difference between cannelloni and ravioli.

20 Name four dishes using pasta as a garnish.

21 What does gnocchi mean?
    pasta; gnome; bun; dumpling

22 Name three types of gnocchi and state the main ingredient of each.

23 Why is it necessary to simmer gnocchi gently?

24 Name three different types of rice and state the type of dishes each are best suited for.

25 What is the approximate cooking time for long-grained rice?

26 What is the difference between a pilaff and a risotto?

27 List four points which need particular attention when cooking riz pilaf so as to achieve a good result.

28 Why is long-grained rice used for riz pilaff?

29 Name two savoury rice dishes.

30 Which of the following is not a pasta?
    ravioli; cannelloni; spaghetti italienne; brindisi au beurre

31 Match the appropriate sauce with the correct dish:
    béchamel   spaghetti bolognaise
    tomato   macaroni cheese
    demi-glace   spaghetti napolitaine

32 List six different types of manufactured pasta.

QUESTIONS IN DEPTH

1 Name the flour and other ingredients used in making a pasta dough.

2 Why should cooked rice not be kept warm for long periods of time?

3 **a** What is the difference between:
        i ravioli; **ii** cannelloni; **iii** lasagne?
        Describe a typical filling for cannelloni.

   b What is the most suitable rice for a pilaff?
Name and describe two dishes using pilaff. What is the
difference between a pilaff and risotto?

SHORT QUESTIONS – **ANSWERS** _____

1 any of a wide variety of dishes using a dough made from strong wheat flour   *p128 PC*

2 'with a bite', an indication that the pasta should have a slight chew and not be soft and mushy   *p128 PC*

3 less

4 spinach, tomato, saffron, beetroot, etc.   *p130 PC*

5 dishes containing flour or with a high starch content

6 pasta

7 false – any meal or snack time with the exception of breakfast

8 to prevent the strands from sticking together

9 cheese

10 plenty of boiling salted water, stir to the boil etc.   *p129 PC*

11 e.g. spaghetti with tomato sauce; macaroni cheese etc.   *pp131–140 PC*

12 Parmesan

13 tomato

14 Ham   *p136 PC*

15 Semolina   *p134 PC*

16 minced beef

17 narrow strips   *p134 PC*

18 false, a noodle type paste is used

19 canneloni – filled tubes
ravioli – savoury mixture sealed in paste   *p139 PC*

20 e.g. braised beef with noodles; veal goulash; veal escalope napolitaine

21 dumpling

22   e.g. parisienne – choux paste; romaine – semolina; piemontaise –
potato   *pp141–142 PC*

23   otherwise they will break up

24   long grain – savoury dishes
short grain – sweet dishes
Basmati – Indian dishes
Arborio – risotto   *p143 PC*

25   12–15 minutes

26   pilaff – braised in oven with all liquid added at the start   *p144 PC*
risotto – cooked on top of stove with liquid gradually added
p145 PC

27   e.g. correct type of rice; careful measurement; controlled cooking
time; remove from cooking pan immediately

28   because it has a firm structure and retains its shape

29   braised rice with mushrooms; risotto

30   brindisi au beurre

31   béchamel – macaroni cheese; tomato – spaghetti napolitaine;
demi-glace – spaghetti bolognaise

32   e.g. spaghetti, macaroni, tagliatelle, lasagne, riccioli

QUESTIONS IN DEPTH – **OUTLINE ANSWERS**

1   durum flour, olive oil, water and eggs   *p130 PC*

2   because of the spores of a bacterium (bacillus cereus) which may
revert to bacteria, multiply and produce a toxin   *p143 PC*

3   **a**   **i** filled pasta envelopes;   **ii** filled pasta rolls;   **iii** layered
sheets of pasta with a filling
braised beef, spinach, onion, garlic, seasoning, herbs
pp138–139 PC

   b   long grained rice, e.g. riz pilaff aux champignons – sweated
onion, rice; mushrooms cooked in stock in oven
pilaff cooked in oven, all stock added at once
risotto cooked on stove, stock gradually added during cooking
pp144–145 PC

FISH AND SHELLFISH

CHAPTER 8

Read pp 147–181 of *Practical Cookery*.

SHORT QUESTIONS

1   Give three examples of white fish.

2   Which is the odd one and why?
      halibut; hake; herring; haddock

3   Name three shellfish.

4   List five quality points for fish.

5   Which is suitable for boiling?
      sprats; sole; salmon; herring

6   Explain how fish are boiled.

7   What is a court bouillon?
      royal stock; boiling kettle; fish stock; liquid for cooking oily
      fish

8   What are the ingredients used in the making of a court bouillon?

9   Explain how fish are poached.

10   What term is applied to shallow fried fish?
      sauté; goujons; darne; meunière

11   What is the reason for selecting a specific side to be cooked first
      when shallow-frying fillets of fish?
      appearance is better; cooks more evenly; cooks more quickly;
      portion looks larger

12   Which side of a fillet is placed in the fat first when being shallow
      fried?

13   Describe three coatings for deep fried fish and explain the reason
      for coating fish before deep frying.

14   How should fresh fish be stored?

15 At what temperature should frozen fish be stored?

16 Name four fish that are canned.

17 What is caviar?

18 What are rollmops?

19 Where should smoked fish be stored?

20 Name three cuts of fish suitable for roasting.

21 Why is it best to purchase shellfish alive wherever possible?

22 What is the effect on the flesh of lobster if overboiled?

23 What is the difference between crawfish and lobster?

24 State four uses for crab meat.

25 How should mussels be stored?

26 Give four different ways of using mussels.

27 Suggest three ways of cooking scallops.

28 How much fish is allowed per portion on the bone; and off the bone?

29 What is fish velouté used for?
       fish stock; fish glaze; fish sauces; fish cocktail

30 What is the base for a sabayon?
       uncooked yolks; cooked whites; cooked whole eggs;
       uncooked whole eggs

31 Why may a sabayon be used in a fish sauce?

32 How is a sabayon made?

33 What care must be taken when making a sabayon?

34 Which flat fish is skinned before being filleted?

35 How would fillets of plaice meunière be finished for serving?

36 What is garnish belle meunière?
       shrimp, tomato, herring roe; mushrooms, tomato, shrimp;
       mushrooms, shrimps, herring roe; mushrooms, tomato,
       herring roe

37 Suggest three variations for fish meunière.

38   Explain the preparation of herring for grilling.

39   How is grilled fish finished and presented for service?

40   What would mustard sauce be served with?
soused herrings; grilled herrings; shallow fried herrings; deep fried herrings

41   Name three raising agents that may be used in frying batters.

42   Compile a list of six points to ensure safety when deep frying fish.

43   Describe how deep fried fish is served.

44   Which sauce may be served with crumbed deep fried fish?
egg; tartar; parsley; demi glace

45   How are whiting prepared for frying?

46   What size are filets de sole en goujons and why are they so called?

47   The marinade for fried fish à l'Orly consists of . . . ?

48   What is the temperature of the fat in which whitebait are cooked?
105°C; 125°C; 175°C; 195°C

49   Whitebait are served with their heads on: true/false.

50   What is the English term for young turbot?

51   Describe the difference in shape between brill and turbot.

52   Which of the following accompanies hot cooked salmon?
sliced cucumber; grated cheese; grated carrot; sliced truffle

53   Name three white fish which may be used for boiling.

54   When cooking whole fish in a liquid, why should the liquid be only allowed to simmer gently?

55   When poaching fish why is only the minimum of liquid used?

56   What is served with a fish dish named Véronique?
bananas; oranges; grapes; apples

57   What is kedgeree?

58   Which fish is sometimes served with black butter and capers?
halibut; plaice; skate; salmon

59   What method of cookery is employed for cooking the dish in Question 58?

60 Suggest three ways of using cooked fish.

61 If half a lobster is served for a portion, a 1kg (2lb) lobster would be ordered: true/false.

62 Explain the significance of using the words *fillet* and *fillets* on the menu.

63 How should mussels be prepared prior to cooking?
      salted and drained; washed and filleted; blanched and
      drained; scraped and washed

64 Why should the raw mussel shells be tightly closed?

65 How may scallop shells be opened?
      on top of the stove; in boiling water; under the salamander;
      in a steamer

66 What sort of potato is piped round the edge of a scallop shell for scallop with cheese sauce?
      mashed; duchess; purée; creamed

QUESTIONS IN DEPTH

1 a What are the two main groups of fish? Give three examples for each and outline their respective food value.
   b When purchasing, what are the signs of quality to look for?
   c Name the two main groups of shellfish with three examples of each.
   d What is the difference in method between skinning plaice fillets and Dover sole? Give two popular menu examples for the use of each.

2 a Name seven ways of cooking fish and give a menu example for each.
   b Give examples of liquids in which fish can be boiled or poached, the ingredients for a court-bouillon for oily fish; name and describe six cuts of fish.
   c What is the chief purpose of coating fish before deep frying? Name three different coatings and examples of fish cooked by each.
   d Give the procedure for baking fish and give two menu examples.

3 a Give the method for shallow frying fish and suggest three variations as they would appear on a menu. Why is it essential to fry presentation side first?

b What is the difference between the preparation for the
following?
i grilling herring;   **ii** mackerel

c What would be the approximate difference in temperature °C
between deep frying a Dover sole and whitebait, and why?

d Suggest three hot dishes which include the use of cooked fish
and potato.

4 Name four ways of preserving fish and give two examples in each
case.

5 Name six fish preserved by smoking.

6 Give the procedure for roasting a piece of fish.

7 How are raw and cooked prawns prepared?

8 Suggest a modern presentation for grilled sea bass.

SHORT QUESTIONS – ANSWERS

1 e.g. plaice, cod, whiting   *p149 PC*

2 herring because it is an oily fish, the others are white   *p149 PC*

3 e.g. crab mussels, prawns   *p175 PC*

4 eyes bright, gills red, flesh firm, plentiful scales, smell   *p149 PC*

5 salmon

6 immersed in liquid and gently simmered   *p167 PC*

7 liquid for cooking oily fish

8 water, vegetables, herbs, seasoning, vinegar

9 fish barely covered with fish stock and buttered paper, gently
brought to the boil, cooked in oven or steamer   *p167 PC*

10 meunière   *p158 PC*

11 appearance is better   *p158 PC*

12 presentation side

13 batter; milk and flour; flour; egg and crumb; to prevent fat
penetrating into fish   *pp164–165 PC*

14 in a separate refrigerator or fish box containing ice

15 minus 18°C (0°F) *p149 PC*

16 sardines; salmon; tuna; anchovies *p150 PC*

17 salted roe of sturgeon *p150 PC*

18 rolled pickled herring *p150 PC*

19 in a refrigerator

20 steaks of salmon, turbot and monkfish *p155 PC*

21 to ensure freshness

22 it toughens the meat *p175 PC*

23 crawfish only have flesh in the tail *pp175–176 PC*

24 salad; sandwiches; cocktail; fish cakes *p177 PC*

25 in containers covered with damp seaweed in refrigerator *p178 PC*

26 soups; salads; sauces; garnishes *p178 PC*

27 poached; grilled; fried *p179 PC*

28 on bone 150g (6oz); off bone 100g (4oz)

29 fish sauces

30 uncooked yolks *p156 PC*

31 to enrich and assist glazing

32 whisking egg yolks and water over gentle heat *p156 PC*

33 not to overcook or scramble the eggs

34 Dover sole *p153 PC*

35 with lemon juice, nut brown butter and parsley *p158 PC*

36 mushrooms, tomato, herring roe *p158 PC*

37 lemon segments and capers; cucumber; shrimps and mushrooms *p158 PC*

38 descale, clean, wash, dry, incise, flour, oil *p160 PC*

39 garnish with lemon, picked parsley, accompanying sauce *p160 PC*

40 grilled herrings

41 yeast, beaten egg whites (air); beaten eggs (air)

42   e.g. not overfilling fryer; dry food; not overloading fryer with
     food; careful handling   *p38 PC*

43   garnish with picked parsley, lemon and/or suitable sauce *p154 PC*

44   tartar

45   picked, washed, drained, floured   *p165 PC*

46   size approx 8cm × ½cm (3in × ¼in) – named after a small fish
     called gudgeon   *p155 PC*

47   oil, lemon juice, chopped parsley, seasoning   *p166 PC*

48   195°C   *p167 PC*

49   true

50   chicken turbot

51   turbot is almost round, brill elongated

52   sliced cucumber

53   e.g. turbot, brill, cod   *p167 PC*

54   otherwise the fish may break up

55   to conserve flavour in the cooking liquid which is used in the
     coating sauce   *p168 PC*

56   grapes   *p170 PC*

57   pilaf rice, flaked fish, hard boiled eggs, curry sauce   *p172 PC*

58   skate   *p172 PC*

59   poached in a court bouillon   *p172 PC*

60   fish cakes; pie; bouchées

61   false, usually half a ½kg (1lb) lobster

62   fillet should indicate one piece of fish; fillets should indicate two
     or more

63   scraped and washed   *p178 PC*

64   because this signifies they are alive. When dead the shells open and
     should be discarded.   *p178 PC*

65   on top of the stove   *p179 PC*

66   duchess

QUESTIONS IN DEPTH – **OUTLINE ANSWERS** _____

1   a   white e.g. plaice (flat), cod (round)
           oily e.g. mackerel
           Fish has good protein equal to meat. Oily fish contains
           vitamins A and D in the flesh – in certain white fish, only in
           the liver e.g. cod   *p149 PC*
      b   eyes, gills, flesh, scales, smell   *p149 PC*
      c   crustacea e.g. crab; mollusca e.g. mussels   *p175 PC*
      d   plaice is filleted before skinning, and sole is skinned before
           filleting   *p153 PC*
           e.g. fried fillets of plaice, tartare sauce
           fillets of sole bonne-femme

2   a   boiling, poaching, steaming, grilling, shallow frying, deep
           frying, baking

Menu examples

> Grilled salmon, herb sauce
> River trout shallow fried
> with lemon and capers
> Deep fried fillets of plaice in batter,
> tomato sauce
> Poached turbot,
> egg and butter sauce

      b   e.g. water and milk, fish stock
           courtbouillon – water, vinegar, vegetables, herbs
           e.g. darne – slice of round fish on bone; tronçon – slice of flat
           fish on bone   *pp153–154 PC*
      c   to prevent fat penetration
           e.g. flour, egg and breadcrumbs – fried breadcrumbed fillets of
           sole – milk and flour – devilled whitebait – batter – fried fillet
           of codling, tartar sauce   *pp165–166 PC*
      d   baked whole, portioned or filleted with a savoury stuffing,
           cooked in ovenproof dish with vegetables, herbs e.g. baked sea
           bass   *C*

3   a   flour, shallow fry both sides, finish with lemon, parsley, nut
           brown butter
           e.g. fillet of turbot with shrimps and mushrooms
           fat is clean, giving good presentation   *pp154–158 PC*

b i herring – whole, cut incision in flesh, pass through
seasoned flour

ii mackerel – opened and boned, pass through seasoned
flour

c 20°C; whitebait being much smaller require hotter fat as they
cook more quickly

d e.g. fish cakes, fish pie

4 freezing – e.g. cod, plaice
canning – e.g. sardines, pilchards
salting – e.g. herring, caviar
pickling – e.g. rollmops, cockles   *p150 PC*

5 e.g. haddock, bloaters, herring, eel, kippers, salmon, cod

6 take a thick cut of turbot, lightly brush with oil and season. Place
in a roasting tray, add finely sliced vegetables, herbs and cook in
oven. Deglaze tray with white wine   *p155 PC*

7 remove heads, carapace, legs, tail section and dark intestinal veins,
wash if necessary   *p175 PC*

8 Grilled sea bass with red onion confit   *p161 PC*

MEAT AND POULTRY

CHAPTER 9

Lamb and mutton

Read pp 182–210 of *Practical Cookery*.

SHORT QUESTIONS

1 Approximately how much lamb on the bone and how much off the bone is calculated per head when ordering?

2 What is the difference between lamb and mutton?

3 Name the joints in a carcass of lamb.

4 List the points which indicate quality in lamb.

5 List the small cuts of lamb.

6 State from which joints the small cuts are obtained.

7 The tail end of the saddle is called the . . .

8 A saddle divided into two lengthwise produces two . . .

9 When skinning a saddle it is best to skin from tail to head and back to breast: true/false.

10 Why is the surface of the saddle of lamb scored?
    for ease of carving; to allow fat to flow out; to shorten cooking time; to assist basting

11 How are noisettes of lamb prepared?

12 List the offal obtained from a carcass of lamb.

13 Which joints of lamb may be cooked by roasting?

14 Name two kinds of lamb chops.

15 Which lamb joints are suitable for stuffing?
    leg; shoulder; best end; loin

16 Which sauce is traditionally served with roast lamb?

17   Which sauce is traditionally served with roast mutton?
       onion; cranberry; horseradish; apple

18   Which jelly is traditionally served with roast mutton?
       cranberry; orange; quince; redcurrant

19   The best end is cut into chops; true/false.

20   List the usual ingredients in a mixed grill.

21   Describe the preparation of lamb cutlets for cutlets reform.

22   What sauce is traditionally served with boiled leg of mutton?
       parsley; caper; egg; mushroom

23   From what liquor is this sauce made?

24   What are kebabs, how are they cooked, and with what are they
       usually served?

25   What kind of fish could be used for kebabs?

26   Suggest three ways of serving lamb chops.

27   Describe four suitable garnishes for serving with noisette of lamb.

28   What is the filet mignon?
       the top of the leg; the equivalent joint to the nut of veal; the
       equivalent joint to the fillet of beef; boned out shoulder

29   Name four different varieties of lamb stew.

30   What do the words *navarin* and *ragoût* indicate?

31   What does 'turned' mean when applied to vegetables?
       shaped like a barrel; shaken in the pan; canned vegetables;
       finished in butter

32   How are turned glazed vegetables produced?

33   Long grain rice is used for plain boiled rice: true/false.

34   What points distinguish high standards for plain boiled rice?

35   How is a high standard of plain boiled rice achieved?

36   List a selection of items which may accompany curried lamb.

37   Bombay duck is roasted: true/false.

38   Describe poppadums and explain how they are cooked and served.

39   What is moussaka?

40 From what country does moussaka originate?
Italy; Russia; Turkey; Greece

41 Suggest three dishes using cooked lamb.

42 Name four items of lamb offal and suggest a suitable dish for each.

43 Why must sautéd kidneys be drained after being fried?
to prevent loss of juices; to remove strong flavour; to increase
flavour; to shrink them

44 From which joints are cutlets and chops obtained?

QUESTIONS IN DEPTH

1 **a** What are the signs of quality in a carcass of lamb?
b Name three prime joints suitable for roasting and three
suitable for stewing. Give three menu examples of lamb stew.
c Name three lamb joints that can be boned and stuffed. Give
the recipe for a suitable stuffing.
d Name four items of lamb offal and give a menu description for
each.

2 **a** When roasting lamb, why should joints be raised from the
roasting pan by means of a trivet? What can happen to a joint
if it is carved immediately it is cooked and what is the remedy?
b Give the methods for making roast gravy.
c Give two names for pieces of lamb cooked on a skewer.
Suggest items of food that can be cooked along with the lamb.
How may different flavours be introduced?
d Suggest and give method for two lamb dishes prepared from
cooked meat.

SHORT QUESTIONS – ANSWERS

1 on bone 150g (6oz) – off bone 100g (4oz)   *p196 PC*

2 lamb is under 12 months old   *p188 PC*

3 shoulder; leg; breast; middle neck; scrag end; best end   *p187 PC*

4 compact; evenly fleshed; firm lean flesh; colour of flesh and fat;
bone structure   *p188 PC*

5 e.g. chops; cutlets; fillet   *p188 PC*

6 e.g. chops from loin; chumps; cutlets from best end   *pp189–190 PC*

7   the chump end   *p190 PC*

8   loins   *p189 PC*

9   false, always skin from head to tail and breast to back   *p189 PC*

10 to allow fat to flow out

11 cut on the slant from boned loin   *p190 PC*

12 e.g. kidney; heart; liver   *p191 PC*

13 e.g. leg; loin; shoulder   *p191 PC*

14 loin; chump   *p189 PC*

15 shoulder; loin   *pp188–189 PC*

16 mint   *p192 PC*

17 onion   *p192 PC*

18 redcurrant   *p192 PC*

19 false, it is cut into cutlets   *p190 PC*

20 cutlet; kidney; sausage; bacon; tomato; mushroom   *p193 PC*

21 pass prepared cutlets through seasoned flour, eggwash and
    breadcrumbs containing chopped ham and parsley   *p195 PC*

22 caper

23 the cooking liquor from the joint

24 slices of meat and vegetables on a skewer which are cooked by
    grilling and served with rice   *p196 PC*

25 firm fish e.g. monkfish   *p196 PC*

26 braised; grilled; fried

27 e.g. tomatoes filled with jardinière of vegetables and château
    potatoes; balls of cauliflower Mornay and château potatoes
                                                                    p197 PC

28 equivalent joint to the fillet of beef

29 e.g. Navarin; curry; Irish; blanquette   *pp199–203 PC*

30 brown stew   *p199 PC*

31 shaped like a barrel

32 turn or cut in even pieces, cook in minimum water, finally toss
    over heat in butter   *p221 PC*

33 true

34 not overcooked, rice grains not sticking together

35 pick and wash, add to boiling salted water, stir to boil, simmer
    gently, wash well, drain on a sieve, cover with a cloth   *p201PC*

36 e.g. chutney; desiccated coconut; diced cucumber in yoghurt;
    chopped apple; sultanas   *p201 PC*

37 false, it is grilled   *p201 PC*

38 thin vegetable wafers, grilled or deep fried, served as
    accompaniment to curry dishes   *p201 PC*

39 a dish of Eastern Mediterranean origin, minced lamb, aubergines,
    tomatoes etc.   *p207 PC*

40 Greece   *p207 PC*

41 moussaka; shepherds pie; minced lamb

42 liver – fried liver and bacon   *pp208–210 PC*
    hearts – braised lambs' hearts
    kidneys – grilled kidneys and bacon
    sweetbreads – sweetbread escalopes with mushrooms

43 to remove strong unpleasant flavour contained in the juice

44 cutlets from best end; chops from loin and chump   *p189 PC*

QUESTIONS IN DEPTH – **OUTLINE ANSWERS**

1   a   compact, evenly fleshed, lean meat – colour, texture, grain –
        fat even, hard, brittle, flaky, white – bones pink, porous
                                                             p188 PC

    b   roasting – leg, saddle, best end, loin
        stewing – shoulder, middle neck, breast
        e.g. lamb stew with spring vegetables – Irish stew

    c   shoulder, breast, loin
        combine chopped suet, onion, herbs, breadcrumbs and egg
                                                           pp187–191 PC

    d   e.g. hearts – braised; kidneys – grilled with bacon   *p191 PC*

2   **a**   to stop bottom surface from frying and becoming hard, slices
tend to shrink and curl – rest for 10–15 mins   *p191 PC*

b   remove joint, allow sediment to settle, strain off fat, brown
sediment, deglaze with stock, simmer, season, colour, strain,
degrease   *p192 PC*

c   shish kebab, lamb brochette
mushrooms, peppers (red, yellow), onion, bay leaves
marinading in oil, herbs etc.   *p196 PC*

d   e.g. shepherds pie – cooked chopped onion, minced lamb,
seasoning, sauce in a dish topped with mashed potato and
browned   *p206 PC*
Moussaka – cooked chopped onions, minced lamb, seasoning,
sauce in dish, layers of aubergine, tomato, breadcrumbs,
cheese, browned or béchamel with eggs   *p207 PC*

Beef

Read pp 211–235 of *Practical Cookery Ninth Edition.*

SHORT QUESTIONS

1   Name the joints in a hindquarter of beef.

2   Name the joints in a forequarter of beef.

3   List the points of quality in beef.

4   Suggest a suitable order for dissecting a hindquarter.

5   What is brine?

6   What is brine used for?
salting silverside of beef; straining beef stock; seasoning beef
stews; shrinking string on beef

7   Name the small cuts of beef obtained from sirloin.

8   Name the four cuts on a fillet of beef.

9   Name the offal obtained from a carcass of beef.

10   Which is the most suitable joint for roasting?
silverside; chuck steak; thick flank; sirloin

11   What are the traditional accompaniments for roast beef?

12   State the points which indicate when a joint of beef is cooked.

13   Which vegetables are served with French style boiled beef?

14   Which two items usually accompany boiled beef French style?

>   capers and coarse salt; pickled red cabbage and French
>   mustard; pickled gherkins and coarse salt; pickled gherkins
>   and French mustard

15   Name six steaks and state from which joint they are obtained.

16   Name four degrees of grilling steaks.

17   What is the usual garnish served with grilled steak?

18   Roast gravy is served with grilled meat: true/false.

19   A point steak is cut from which of the following?
>   sirloin; wing rib; fillet; rump

20   Suggest four ways of serving sautéd tournedos.

21   Why is a brown beef stew served in an entrée dish?

22   Which of the following would be used in a beef stew with red
     wine?
>   hock; chablis; claret; marsala

23   Which of the following cuts would be used for beef Stroganoff?
>   fillet; topside; thick flank; sirloin

24   Why is this cut chosen for beef Stroganoff?

25   Which of the following is an ingredient for carbonnade of beef?
>   vichy water; wine; beer; cider

26   Which of the following is used in goulash?
>   paprika; pimento; cayenne; cinnamon

27   Goulash is garnished with gnocchi: true/false.

28   What is the English for paupiettes of beef?

29   Before serving paupiettes the . . . must be removed.

30   Name two cuts of beef suitable for braising.

31   Is braised beef cut with the grain or across the grain?

32   What is the reason for the answer to Question 31?

33   How is a joint of braised beef tested to see if it is cooked?

34 Suggest three suitable garnishes for braised beef.

35 Which paste is used for making dumplings?
          suet; short; choux; noodle

36 How may minced beef be presented in an attractive manner?

37 Which kind of meat is used to make Vienna steaks?
          lean minced beef; lean minced lamb; cooked meat; venison

38 What is the correct shape for croquettes, cutlets and Vienna
          steaks?

39 Which wine is usually added to the sauce served with braised ox
          tongue?
          Madeira; Marsala; sherry; port

40 An ox tongue will cook in approximately how long?
          1–2 hours; 2–3 hours; 3–4 hours; 4–5 hours

41 Braised ox liver requires approximately . . . hours simmering to
          become tender.

42 400g (1lb) of tripe to 200g (½lb) onions are needed to produce
          four portions: true/false.

43 Which pulse is sometimes used to garnish oxtail?
          lentils; butter beans; haricot beans; yellow split peas

44 What is the approximate cooking time for oxtail?

45 What is the price of fillet of beef?

46 What is the cost of oxtail?

47 Is ox liver more expensive than lamb's liver?

48 How much does minced beef cost?

49 Which fish could be used as an additional variation in steak and
          kidney pudding?

QUESTIONS IN DEPTH

1   **a**   Name the points of quality to look for in beef.
    b   Excluding the fillet, name six joints from a hindquarter of beef
              and give two menu examples for the use of each.
    c   **i**   List the cuts and various uses of a fillet of beef.
              ii Give two different menu examples.

d Describe the following:
minute steak; entrecôte steak; double entrecôte steak; porterhouse; T-bone steak

2 **a** Name six items of beef offal and give a menu description for the use of each.

b Name the four prime roasting joints of beef, give the approximate cooking times and the accompaniments.

c What is the essential difference between boiled beef English style and boiled beef French style? Name the usual joint and additional ingredients used in the cooking of each.

d What do you understand by:
i beef Stroganoff; **ii** goulash; **iii** carbonnade; **iv** paupiettes

SHORT QUESTIONS – **ANSWERS** _____

1 shin; topside; silverside; thick flank; rump; sirloin; wing ribs; thin flank; fillet *p212PC*

2 fore rib; middle rib; chuck rib; sticking piece; plate; brisket; leg of mutton cut; shank *p213 PC*

3 lean meat red and marbled, firm brittle fat *p214 PC*

4 remove rump and kidney, remove thick flank, divide loin and rump from remainder, remove fillet etc. *p212 PC*

5 preserving solution of water, salt, saltpetre, aromates *p214 PC*

6 salting silverside of beef

7 sirloin steaks and fillet steaks *p215 PC*

8 Chateaubriand; fillet steak; tournedos; mignon *p215 PC*

9 tongue; heart; liver; tripe; kidney; sweetbreads *p216 PC*

10 sirloin

11 Yorkshire pudding; roast gravy; horseradish sauce

12 a little blood issuing from the meat when pressed *p217 PC*

13 celery, leek, cabbage, onions, carrots, turnips *p218 PC*

14 pickled gherkins and coarse salt *p218 PC*

15 rump – rump; fillet – fillet; point – rump; tournedos – fillet; minute – sirloin; porterhouse – sirloin *pp215–216 PC*

16   rare; underdone; just done; well done   *p222 PC*

17   watercress, deep-fried potato, a suitable sauce e.g. béarnaise or
     parsley butter   *p222 PC*

18   false – usually béarnaise, devilled sauce or parsley or garlic butter

19   rump

20   sauce chasseur; mushroom sauce; sauce bordelaise; rossini –
     topped with foie gras, truffle, coated with madeira sauce

21   so that the meat and sauce remain compact and keeps fresh and
     moist. If served on a flat dish both could dry out before being served

22   claret

23   fillet

24   because of its tenderness

25   beer   *p209 PC*

26   paprika   *p227 PC*

27   true   *p227 PC*

28   beef olives   *p232 PC*

29   strings   *p232 PC*

30   topside; thick flank   *p212 PC*

31   across the grain   *p230 PC*

32   because a neater, more tender slice is achieved

33   when penetrated with a trussing needle no sign of blood should
     issue   *p230 PC*

34   noodles; mixed vegetables; mushrooms   *p230 PC*

35   suet   *p231 PC*

36   serve as minced lambin a border of lightly browned duchess
     potato   *p206 PC*

37   lean minced beef   *p233 PC*

38   croquettes – 5cm (2in) long thick rolls
     Vienna steaks – round thick patties

39   Madeira   *p234 PC*

40   3–4 hours   *p234 PC*

41   1½–2 hours   *p235 PC*

42   true

43   haricot beans   *p235 PC*

44   approximately 3 hours   *p235 PC*

45   current market price

46   current market price

47   no

48   current market price

49   oysters

QUESTIONS IN DEPTH – **OUTLINE ANSWERS** _____

1   a   lean meat, pleasing red, flecks of fat; fat firm, brittle creamy
        white, odourless   *p214 PC*
    b   wing rib e.g. roast ribs of beef, Yorkshire pudding
        topside e.g. beef olives
        thick flank e.g. braised steaks
        shin e.g. consommé
        sirloin e.g. minute steak, garlic butter
        rump e.g. grilled rump steak, béarnaise sauce   *p212 PC*
    c   i   Chateaubriand; fillet steak; tournedos; mignon (tail); fillet
            (joint); chain   *p215 PC*
        ii e.g. grilled fillet   *p222 PC*
            e.g. beef Stroganoff (tail end)   *p226 PC*
    d   minute steak – thin cuts from sirloin, flattened so steak cooks
        in a minute
        entrecôte steak – thicker cuts from sirloin
        double entrecôte steak – doublesize of sirloin steak
        porterhouse – cut from rib end of sirloin including bone
        T-bone steak – cut from rump end of sirloin including bone
        and fillet   *p215 PC*

2   a   heart e.g. braised ox heart; liver e.g. liver and onions;
        kidneys e.g. stewed beef kidney and mushrooms;
        sweetbreads e.g. braised veal sweetbreads with vegetables;
        tail e.g. braised oxtail; tripe e.g. tripe and onions

    b   sirloin, wing ribs, fore ribs, fillet
         approx 15 minutes per lb plus 15 minutes
         gravy, Yorkshire pudding, horseradish sauce

    c   English – meat salted – silverside, thin or thick flank; carrots, onions, dumplings
         French – meat unsalted – brisket; onions, carrots, turnips, celery, leeks, cabbage   *p218 PC*

    d **i**   strips of beef fillet sautéd in sauce of shallots, cream, wine, lemon served with pilaff rice   *p226 PC*
        ii traditional Hungarian dish of stewed beef flavoured with paprika   *p227 PC*
        iii traditional Belgian dish of thin steaks stewed in beer with onions, sugar and tomato   *p229 PC*
        iv thin slices of beef, stuffed and braised – beef olives   *p232 PC*

Veal

Read pp 236–250 of *Practical Cookery*.

SHORT QUESTIONS

1   Name the joints in a carcass of veal.

2   How much is the average weight of a Dutch milk fed leg of veal?
      9–12kg (18–24lb); 15–18kg (30–36lb); 21–24kg (42–48lb)

3   The proportion of bone in a leg of veal is approximately:
      7%; 14%; 21%; 28%

4   The proportion of meat in a leg of veal suitable for escalopes is:
      20%; 30%; 36%; 46%

5   Which of the following is used for osso buco?
      leg; loin; breast; knuckle

6   Calves' liver is one of the most suitable livers for frying: true/false.

7   The corresponding veal joint to topside of beef is . . .

8   The corresponding veal joint of silverside of beef is . . .

9   The corresponding veal joint to thick flank of beef is . . .

10 When dissecting a leg of veal, the knuckle is removed first: true/false.

11   The anticipated yield on 100g (4oz) escalopes from a 18kg (36lb) leg of veal would be:
        65; 55; 45; 35

12   What colour is the flesh of good quality veal?

13   Flesh of good quality veal should be firm in structure, not soft or flabby: true/false.

14   When preparing osso buco, shin of veal should be cut:
        1–1½cm (½–¾in); 2–3cm (1–1½in); 3–4cm (1½–2in);
        4–6cm (2–3in)

15   Why should veal sweetbreads be well washed, blanched, and trimmed before being used?

16   What is brown veal stew also known as?
        ragoût; navarin; blanquette; fricassée

17   For a blanquette of veal, the meat is cooked in stock: true/false.

18   For a fricassée of veal, the meat is cooked in sauce: true/false.

19   Any white stew of veal may be finished with a liaison of . . .

20   A fricassée of veal may be finished by adding a few drops of lemon juice: true/false.

21   Which of the following pastes would you use to cover a hot veal and ham pie?
        short; rough puff or puff; hot water; choux

22   When preparing a stuffing for veal olives, the finely chopped meat trimmings can be added: true/false.

23   The best veal escalopes are cut from the . . . or . . . of veal?

24   Which of the following is most suitable for frying veal escalopes?
        lard; margarine; olive oil; oil and butter

25   Which of the following veal escalopes would be garnished with a fried egg and anchovy fillets?
        viennoise; napolitaine; Holstein

26   Veal escalopes with cream are pané (flour, egg and crumbed): true/false.

27   Veal escalopes with Madeira are lightly floured before cooking: true/false.

28 What additions are usually made when roasting a leg of veal in order to increase flavour?

29 Roast gravy served with veal is traditionally thin or thickened?

30 Traditional garnish with roast leg of veal is:
    parsley and thyme stuffing and thinly sliced ham; sage and onion stuffing and thinly sliced ham; parsley and chive stuffing and chipolata sausage; parsley and thyme stuffing and chipolata sausage

31 Veal stuffing traditionally contains chopped suet: true/false.

32 Which of the following is more traditionally used in the cooking of osso buco?
    Marsala; red wine; Madeira; dry white wine

33 Which of the following is usually served with calf's liver and bacon?
    tomato sauce; mustard sauce; devilled sauce; jus lié

34 What are sweetbreads and what are their proper names?
    glands; muscles; nerves; joints

35 Which sweetbread is of superior quality, throat or stomach?

36 Veal sweetbreads may be braised white or brown: true/false.

37 What would be considered a suitable garnish for fried breadcrumbed veal escalopes?
    stuffed tomatoes; grilled bacon; aubergine provençale; asparagus tips

QUESTIONS IN DEPTH

1 **a** What are the points of quality in a carcass of veal and what is an average weight for a leg of prime milk-fed veal?
  b Give a menu example for use of each of the following veal joints/cuts: knuckle, leg, best-end, shoulder.
  c What is the essential difference between a fricassée and a blanquette of veal? Give the ingredients and method for a veal Fricassée and suggest suitable vegetable accompaniments.
  d **i** Name two suitable veal joints for stuffing and roasting.
      ii Give ingredients and method for a veal stuffing.

2 **a** From which joint in a carcass of veal are the best escalopes obtained? Approximately how many 100g (4oz) escalopes could be obtained from an 18kg (36lb) leg?

    b Describe the preparation and serving of three popular breadcrumbed veal escalopes.

    c What is the difference in preparation between a veal escalope for Viennoise and à la crème? What alcoholic liquor can be used to flavour the cream sauce? What is the most simple variation to veal escalope à la crème?

    d **i**   What are sweetbreads?

        ii Which two types are used for cooking?

        iii Which of the two is superior in quality? Describe its shape.

        iv Name and describe three ways of cooking sweetbreads.

        v   What is a veal pojarski?

SHORT QUESTIONS – ANSWERS

1	cushion; under cushion; thick flank; knuckle; shoulder; loin; best end; neck-end; scrag	*p237 PC*
2	18–24kg (36–48lb)	*p237 PC*
3	14%	*p237 PC*
4	46%	*p237 PC*
5	knuckle	*p238 PC*
6	true	
7	cushion	*p238 PC*
8	under cushion	*p238 PC*
9	thick flank	*p238 PC*
10	true	
11	55 × 100g (4oz) escalopes	
12	pale pink	*p239 PC*
13	true	
14	2–3cm (1–1½ins) thick	*p238 PC*
15	to cleanse them thoroughly	*p239 PC*
16	ragoût	*p239 PC*
17	true	
18	true	

19	egg yolks and cream	*p240 PC*
20	true	
21	rough puff or puff	*p242 PC*
22	true	
23	cushion or under cushion	*p244 PC*
24	oil and butter	*p244 PC*
25	Holstein	*p244 PC*
26	false, they are lightly flavoured	
27	true	
28	bed of roots and sprigs of thyme and rosemary	
29	thickened	
30	parsley and thyme stuffing and thinly sliced ham	
31	true	
32	dry white wine	*p248 PC*
33	jus lié	*p249 PC*
34	glands, thymus and pancreas glands	*p249 PC*
35	stomach (heart shaped)	*p249 PC*
36	true	
37	asparagus tips	

QUESTIONS IN DEPTH – OUTLINE ANSWERS _____

1 **a** flesh, pale pink, firm, not flabby
        cut surfaces slightly moist, pinkish bones
        firm, pinkish white fat, firm well covered kidney   *p239 PC*
        18kg (36lb) – 23kg (46lb)   *p237 PC*
   b e.g. osso buco, braised leg of veal, roast stuffed shoulder of veal
   c blanquette – meat cooked in stock
        fricassée – meat cooked in sauce
        for fricassée – set meat in butter without colour, mix in flour,
        cook out, add stock
        when cooked, pick out meat, add sabayon to sauce, lemon juice
        finish parsley, croûtons, button onions and mushrooms
                                        p240 PC

    d **i**   shoulder; breast
        ii   cooked onions; suet; herbs; breadcrumbs   *p247 PC*

2 **a** cushion or nut from the leg; 55   *p238 PC*
    b e.g. escalope of veal viennoise – breadcrumbed
        thinly battened-out slice of veal – flour, egg, crumbed, shallow
        fried, finished slice of lemon, capers, chopped parsley, egg,
        nut-brown butter
    c Viennoise – flour, egg, crumbed; à la crème – floured e.g.
        white wine, sherry
        add mushrooms   *p244 PC*
    d **i**   glands   *p249 PC*
        ii thymus, pancreas
        iii pancreas; heart-shaped
        iv e.g. Braised sweetbreads
            Wash, blanch, refresh sweetbreads. Cook in covered pan
            on bed of roots, herbs and stock. Remove lid when three
            quarters cooked, baste frequently to glaze   *p250 PC*
        v minced veal, egg, cream, breadcrumbs moulded cutlet
           shape shallow fried

Pork and bacon

Read pp 251–267 of *Practical Cookery.*

SHORT QUESTIONS

1   Name the joints in a side of pork.

2   The lean flesh of good quality pork should be pale pink, soft and
     of a fine texture: true/false.

3   In order to be able to carve a leg of pork efficiently, it is not
     necessary to remove the aitch bone before the leg is cooked:
     true/false.

4   When scoring the rind of pork, how far apart should the incisions
     be?
          2mm (⅛in); 1cm (½in); 2cm (1in); 3cm (1½in)

5   Which of the following herbs is traditional for seasoning a boned,
     rolled belly of pork for roasting?
          thyme; parsley; tarragon; sage

6   In an oven at 230–250°C a leg of pork should be roasted for approximately:
>   10 minutes to the ½kg (1lb) and 10 minutes over;
>   15 minutes to the ½kg (1lb) and 15 minutes over;
>   20 minutes to the ½kg (1lb) and 20 minutes over;
>   25 minutes to the ½kg (1lb) and 25 minutes over

7   Roast pork must always be well cooked: true/false.

8   The traditional accompaniments for roast pork are:
>   roast gravy, orange sauce, sage and onion stuffing;
>   roast gravy, apple sauce, parsley and thyme stuffing;
>   roast gravy, prune sauce, sage and parsley stuffing;
>   roast gravy, apple sauce, sage and onion stuffing

9   Traditionally, sage and onion stuffing should be prepared using dripping from the pork joint: true/false.

10   Is a dish of pease-pudding suitable for serving with boiled pork: yes/no.

11   Which of the following sauces is most suitable for serving with a grilled pork chop?
>   tomato; apple; parsley; tartar

12   Which of the following would be cooked in with a dish of pork chops à la flamande?
>   red cabbage; peas; apples; tomatoes

13   Which of the following pork joints is most suitable for barbecues?
>   spare ribs; loin; shoulder; leg

14   Forcemeat is a term given to:
>   numerous mixtures of meats; sausage meat before putting into skins; stuffing for roast pork joints; a mince made from a meat substitute

15   What is the price of a leg of pork per ½kg (1lb)?

16   What is the price of shoulder of pork per ½kg (1lb)?

17   What is the price of loin of pork per ½kg (1lb)?

18   What is the price of spare rib of pork per ½kg (1lb)?

19   Name the joints on a side of bacon.

20   What is the price of prime gammon per ½kg (1lb)?

21   What is the price of back rashers per ½kg (1lb)?

22   What is the price of streaky bacon per ½kg (1lb)?

23   The approximate weight of a gammon is:
        2½kg (5lb); 5kg (10lb); 7½kg (15lb); 10kg (20lb)

24   In assessing quality, the lean of bacon should be a deep pink colour and firm: true/false.

25   In assessing quality, the fat should be white, smooth and not excessive in proportion to the lean: true/false.

26   What is the most popular cut of bacon for frying:
        collar; hock; streaky

27   Gammon rashers for grilling should be cut as thinly as possible: true/false.

28   When preparing hock of bacon for boiling, in order to facilitate carving, it is best to leave all bones in: true/false.

29   What should be considered before soaking a bacon joint before boiling?

30   When boiling bacon allow per ½kg (1lb):
        10 minutes + 10 minutes over; 15 minutes + 15 minutes over; 20 minutes + 20 minutes over; 25 minutes + 25 minutes over;

31   Boiled bacon should be removed from the cooking liquor as soon as it is cooked: true/false.

32   What is the traditional sauce for serving with hot boiled bacon?
        tomato; apple; chestnut; parsley

33   Which of the following accompaniments is most traditional for serving with hot boiled bacon?
        macaroni cheese; mashed turnips; buttered swede; pease-pudding

34   Grilled gammon rashers should only be served for breakfast: true/false.

35   In order to carve a ham efficiently and help to keep the slices intact, it is better to leave the aitch bone in: true/false.

36   Which of the following hams is so prepared that it can be sliced thinly and eaten raw?
        Polish; Danish; Wiltshire; Parma

37   A ham is cut from a side of pork: true/false.

38   A gammon is cut from a side of pork: true/false.

QUESTIONS IN DEPTH

1   a   Name the quality points in pork, name four joints suitable for roasting and give approximate age and weight for a suckling pig.

    b   i   Give approximate time for roasting pork.

        ii   How can the skin be kept crisp and what is the name given to the skin?

        iii   What are the traditional accompaniments to roast pork?

        iv   Give ingredients and method for sage and onion stuffing.

    c   i   What are the quality points for bacon?

        ii   Name the three prime joints for cutting rashers.

    d   Give the preparation and method for boiling bacon, name two suitable joints and give a menu example.

SHORT QUESTIONS – ANSWERS

1	leg; loin; spare rib; belly; shoulder; head	*p252 PC*
2	true	
3	false, removal of the aitch bone assists carving	
4	2cm (1in)	*p252 PC*
5	sage	*p254 PC*
6	25 minutes to the ½kg (1lb) plus 25 minutes	*p254 PC*
7	true	*p251 PC*
8	roast gravy, apple sauce, sage and onion stuffing	*p254 PC*
9	true	
10	yes	
11	apple	
12	red cabbage	
13	spare ribs	*p256 PC*
14	numerous mixture of minced meats	*p259 PC*

15   current market price (find this out)

16   current market price (find this out)

17   current market price (find this out)

18   current market price (find this out)

19   collar; hock; back; streaky; gammon   *p262 PC*

20   current market price (find this out)

21   current market price (find this out)

22   current market price (find this out)

23   7½kg (15lbs)   *p262 PC*

24   true

25   true

26   streaky   *p263 PC*

27   false, they should be cut in fairly thick slices   *p263 PC*

28   false, bones hinder efficient carving

29   the salt content   *p262 PC*

30   25 minutes per lb plus 25 minutes   *p263 PC*

31   false, it should be left to cool in the cooking liquid   *p263 PC*

32   parsley   *p263 PC*

33   pease-pudding   *p263 PC*

34   false, they can be served for any meal

35   false, neater slices are obtained if aitch bone is removed

36   Parma

37   true

38   false, it is cut from a side of bacon

QUESTIONS IN DEPTH – **OUTLINE ANSWERS** _____

1   a   lean flesh, pale pink, firm, fine texture or grain, rind smooth
        leg; loin; spare rib; shoulder
        5–6 weeks; 5–10kg (10–20lbs)   *pp252–254 PC*

b **i** 25 minutes per ½kg (1lb) and 25 minutes over
ii brushing with oil; crackling
iii roast gravy, apple sauce, sage and onion stuffing
iv chopped onions cooked in pork dripping, herbs and white
breadcrumbs *p254 PC*
c **i** not sticky; clean smell; smooth rind
lean meat deep pink and firm, fat – white and smooth
p263 PC

ii back; belly (streaky); gammon
d e.g. leg of pork, belly
soak in cold water if necessary
change water, simmer until cooked, cool in liquid
e.g. boiled bacon, pease pudding, parsley sauce *p263 PC*

Poultry and game

Read pp 267–299 of *Practical Cookery.*

SHORT QUESTIONS

1 The largest chicken suitable for roasting is a capon: true/false.

2 The approximate weight of a baby chicken (poussin) is:
200g (½lb); ½kg (1lb); 1kg (2lb); 1½kg (3lb)

3 List four signs of quality in chicken.

4 What is the price of prime roasting chicken per ½kg (1lb)?

5 What is the price of old boiling fowl per ½kg (1lb)?

6 When preparing a chicken for roasting, the wishbone may be removed in order to facilitate carving: true/false.

7 The traditional method of cutting a chicken into pieces for sauté yields two drumsticks, two thighs, two wings, two breasts and the carcass: true/false.

8 The most suitable weight of chicken for cutting suprêmes is:
¾–1kg (1½–2lb); 1¼–1½kg (2½–3lb); 2–3kg (4–6lb)

9 When preparing suprêmes of chicken is the skin left on or off?

10 Why is it more efficient to remove the wishbone from a chicken before removing the suprêmes?

11   A ballottine is:
> a boned stuffed leg of chicken; a ball shaped chicken cutlet; a brown stew of chicken legs; a kitchen knife for cutting ball shaped pieces

12   List four signs of quality in duck.

13   What is the price of prime duck per ½kg (1lb)?

14   What is the approximate weight of a goose?
> 2kg (4lb); 3kg (6lb); 4kg (8lb); 6kg (12lb)

15   Turkeys are available in weights from 3½–20kg (7–40lb): true/false.

16   Which is the traditional stuffing for turkey?
> breadcrumbs and parsley; forcemeat and sage; sausage meat and chestnuts; breadcrumbs and chestnuts

17   Which are the traditional accompaniments for roast turkey?
> roast gravy, bread sauce, cranberry sauce, chipolatas, bacon;
> roast gravy, white sauce, apple sauce, sausage, ham;
> roast gravy, parsley sauce, tomato sauce, chipolatas, bacon;
> roast gravy, bread sauce, cranberry sauce, ham, bacon

18   Which of the following weights of raw dressed bird are required to yield four good portions of raw chicken?
> ¾–1kg (1½–2lb); 1¼–1½kg (2½–3lb); ½–¾kg (1–1½lb); 2–2½kg (4–5lb)

19   When a roast chicken is cooked there should be slight signs of blood in the juice issuing from it: true/false.

20   When preparing a stuffing for roast chicken the chopped raw chicken liver may be added: true/false.

21   What ingredients are used to make the devil mixture for grilled devilled chicken?

22   How is a chicken spatchcock cooked?
> boiled; fried; roasted; grilled

23   When preparing a jus-lié or demi-glace for use with a chicken sauté, the chicken giblets should not be used as they may taint the sauce: true/false.

24   Which of the following are typical ingredients of chicken sauté chasseur?

mushrooms, bacon, tomatoes; tomatoes, courgettes, parsley;
mushrooms, tomatoes, tarragon; tomatoes, rice, tarragon

25   When cooking pieces of chicken for a sauté, indicate with numbers
     1–4 the order the following are put into the pan, and give the reason:
         thighs; drumsticks; wings; breasts

26   When cooking chicken suprêmes with cream, the suprêmes should
     be lightly floured and cooked in butter with the minimum amount
     of colour: true/false.

27   When preparing chicken suprêmes with asparagus tips it is usual to
     pané the suprêmes: true/false.

28   Which of the following rice dishes is usually served with boiled
     chicken and suprême sauce?
         risotto with short grain rice; risotto with long grain rice; pilaf
         with short grain rice; pilaf with long grain rice

29   Which of the following are typical of chicken à la king?
         red pimento, mushrooms, marsala; green pimento,
         mushrooms, red wine; red pimento, mushrooms, sherry;
         green pimento, mushrooms, white wine

30   When preparing chicken vol-au-vent, the chicken mixture should
     be put into the puff pastry cases well in advance of service in order
     to let the flavour soak into the pastry: true/false.

31   Chicken cutlets must always be deep fried: true/false.

32   When preparing a fricassée of chicken, the pieces of chicken
     should be cooked in with the sauce: true/false.

33   Which of the following are the more usual ingredients in a chicken
     pie?
         mushroom, bacon, hard-boiled egg, parsley; onions, carrots,
         leeks, celery; mushrooms, carrots, hard-boiled egg, sage;
         onions, rosemary, tomatoes, courgettes

34   A chicken salad would normally be accompanied by a mayonnaise
     sauce: true/false.

35   When preparing a curry of chicken, the curry powder should be
     diluted in water and added to the dish for the last few minutes of
     cooking only: true/false.

36   Which of the following is the traditional accompaniment to a
     curry of chicken?

plain boiled rice, raw sliced mushrooms, bacon; pilaf rice, sliced tomatoes, grated cheese; pilaf rice, boiled ham, chutney; plain boiled rice, grilled poppadums and Bombay duck

37   What are the traditional accompaniments for English roast duck?
        sage and onion stuffing, cranberry sauce; thyme and parsley stuffing, cranberry sauce; sage and onion stuffing, apple sauce; thyme and parsley stuffing, apple sauce

38   When preparing orange salad to serve with roast duck, how are the oranges cut?
        segments free from skin and pips; slices with skins and rind on; slices free from skin and pips; quarters with skin and rind on

39   It is not necessary to stone cherries for duckling with cherries: true/false.

40   Which of the following is cooked in with braised duck and peas?
        lardons, button onions, peas; ham, chipolatas, peas; lardons, chipolatas, peas; carrots, turnips, peas

41   Name three ways of using ostrich.

QUESTIONS IN DEPTH

1   a   How is a prepared raw chicken assessed for quality? What are the signs of an old bird?
    b   Describe a chicken suprême and a ballottine, and give two menu examples for each.
    c   Give the average weight of a chicken to be cut for sauté, and name the cut pieces. What is the order in which chicken pieces should be placed in the pan and why? Give menu examples for two chicken sauté dishes.
    d   Name three hot dishes that can be prepared using cooked chicken. What do you understand by:
        i coq au vin; ii devilled; iii spatchcock; iv poussin?

2   a   i   What is the approximate weight variation in turkeys?
        ii   What is the approximate raw weight per portion allowed?
        iii   What preliminary preparation is required to facilitate carving of the breasts?
        iv   What pre-preparation is required for turkey legs?
        v   When roasting in an oven at 200°C–230°C (reg 6–8) what is the approximate cooking time per lb?
        vi   What are the traditional accompaniments to roast turkey?

b **i**   What are the signs of quality in a duck?
   ii   What are the traditional accompaniments to roast duck?
     Give the menu descriptions for three other hot duck
     dishes. Describe the ingredients and service of roast duck
     orange salad.

SHORT QUESTIONS – **ANSWERS** _____

1   true

2   ½kg (1lb)   *p268 PC*

3   plump breast; pliable breast bone; firm flesh; unbroken skin with
   faint blue tint   *p269 PC*

4   current market price

5   current market price

6   true   *p269 PC*

7   true   *p270 PC*

8   1¼–1½kg (2½–3lb)   *p271 PC*

9   off   *p271 PC*

10   because the suprême can then be removed more cleanly and
    efficiently

11   a boned stuffed chicken leg   *p272 PC*

12   plump breast; pliable lower back; easily torn webbed feet; yellow
    feet and bill   *p273 PC*

13   current market price

14   6kg (12lbs)   *p273 PC*

15   true

16   sausage meat and chestnuts

17   roast gravy, bread sauce, cranberry sauce, chipolatas, bacon *p274 PC*

18   1¼–1½kg (3lb)

19   true

20   true

21   mustard, Worcester sauce, cayenne pepper, vinegar

22 grilled   *p278 PC*

23 false, when properly cleaned they assist in giving flavour to a sauce

24 mushrooms, tomatoes, tarragon   *p278 PC*

25 drumsticks, thighs, wings, breasts: in this order the toughest
    pieces are cooked first. If all pieces were cooked at the same time
    the tender pieces (wings, breasts) could be overcooked   *p277 PC*

26 true

27 true

28 pilaf with long grain rice

29 red pimento, mushroom, sherry   *p284 PC*

30 false, the chicken should be placed into pre-warmed puff pastry
    cases at the last moment in order to keep them crisp

31 false, they may be shallow or deep fried

32 true

33 mushroom, bacon, hard-boiled egg, parsley   *p288 PC*

34 it could be, but a vinaigrette would be more usual

35 false, the curry powder should be cooked in with the chicken from
    the beginning   *p289 PC*

36 plain boiled rice, grilled poppadums, Bombay duck   *p289 PC*

37 sage and onion stuffing, apple sauce   *p291 PC*

38 segments free from skin and pips   *p292 PC*

39 false

40 lardons, button onions, peas

41 Stir fry, paupietes, grilled   *p297 PC*

QUESTIONS IN DEPTH – **OUTLINE ANSWERS** _____

1   a   plump breast, pliable breast bone, firm flesh, unbroken white
        skin, faint bluish tint
        an old bird has coarse leg scales, large spurs, long hairs on skin
                                                                    p269 PC

    b   suprême – wing and half the chicken breast with trimmed wing bone attached; e.g. crumbed wing and breast of chicken with mushrooms   *p271 PC*
ballottine – boned, stuffed leg, e.g. chicken ballotine chasseur – boned, stuffed leg of chicken with tomatoes, mushrooms and white wine sauce   *p272 PC*

    c   1¼–1½kg (2½–3lbs); drumstick, wing etc.   *p270 PC*
tougher pieces first e.g. drumstick   *p277 PC*
e.g. chicken sauté with mushrooms

    d   Chicken vol-au-vent; chicken in creamy sauce with pimentoes, glazed; chicken croquettes

       i   chicken in red wine   *p290 PC*
       ii devilled, usually refers to a method of grilling chicken
       iii method of cutting a chicken for grilling   *p278 PC*
       iv baby chicken   *p268 PC*

2   **a** **i**   3½–20kg (7–40lb)
       ii 200g (½lb)
       iii removal of wishbone
       iv sinews drawn out of legs   *p273 PC*
       v 15–20 minutes per lb
       vi chestnut stuffing, parsley and thyme stuffing, roast gravy, bread sauce, cranberry sauce   *p274 PC*

   b **i**   e.g. plump breast; back bends easily; feet tear easily; bill yellow   *p273 PC*
       ii gravy, apple sauce, stuffing   *p291 PC*
e.g. braised duck with peas – canard braisé aux petit pois; duckling with orange sauce – caneton bigarade   *p292 PC*
duck confit – Confit de canard   *p294 PC*

ETHNIC DISHES

CHAPTER 10

Read pp 300–356 of *Practical Cookery*.

SHORT QUESTIONS

1   What are the benefits in acquiring a knowledge and understanding of Ethnic Cookery?

2   What particular influences affect the eating habits of Muslims, Hindus, Jews and other similar groups?

3   Muslims are traditionally forbidden . . . and . . . and only meat prepared by a . . . butcher is permitted.

4   Why do most Hindus not eat beef?

5   Name two strict ethnic groups who are vegetarians.

6   Give six popular spices used in Asian, Middle Eastern and Far Eastern cookery.

7   What is the Caribbean dish of saltfish with coconut and plantains called?

8   Plantains are large . . .

9   What are the other two unusual vegetables used in Caribbean cookery?

10 Name and briefly describe one Caribbean dish.

11 A wok can be used for stir frying, deep frying and steaming: true/false.

12 What is the essential previous preparation required before starting to cook a Chinese style stir fry dish?

13 Soy sauce is used frequently in Chinese cookery both in marinading and for sauces. What is the basic ingredient of soy sauce?

14 Which of the following oils is used the most in Chinese cookery?
       olive; walnut; sesame seed; maize; ground nut; palm

15 Describe dolmades and give a list of the typical ingredients used.

16 A popular Greek sweet is baked filo pastry with nuts and sugar, which is known as what?

17 Briefly describe a moussaka.

18 When cooking a chicken palak why is it necessary to gently fry the spices?

19 Chicken tikka is marinated in spices, yoghurt, garlic, lemon juice and tomato purée for . . . hours before cooking.

20 Name four spices that can be used when cooking chicken tikka.

21 What is dahl?

22 Describe the consistency of dahl when ready for serving.

23 What is a tandoor?

24 What name is given to foods cooked by this method?

25 If a tandoor is not available what could be used as an alternative?

26 Give a brief description of Gado gado and Nasi goreng.

27 What are the advantages of a wok over a frying pan or saucepan?

28 Tofu is used considerably in Japanese cookery. What is tofu?

29 What is sushi rice?

30 What is the Japanese term for frying fish and other foods dipped in batter?

31 Briefly describe yakitori and teppanyaki.

32 A typical marinade for teppanyaki would consist of five ingredients: soy sauce; sweet . . .; . . . oil; . . . vinegar; . . . sugar.

33 What is sashimi and what is an essential requirement for the food used?

34 Briefly describe the following: tortillas; tostada; tacos; enchiladas; burritos.

35 Name the two basic ingredients of hummus?

36 What other ingredients are used to make hummus?

37 Name the cracked wheat salad often served with hummus, kebabs or spiced lamb.

38   Cous cous is the national dish of which three countries?

39   What is cous cous?

40   Describe the correct way of cooking cous cous?

41   Briefly outline the dietary laws that govern the preparation and serving of kosher foods.

42   What are potato latkes?

43   What is chollo bread?

44   Briefly describe:
         matzo fritters; blitz kuchen; carrot kugel.

45   One of the most traditional and popular Spanish dishes is paella. Give the ingredients used and a brief method of preparation.

46   What is chorizo?

47   When using ground spices in a recipe, how is the maximum flavour best extracted?

48   What is garam masala?

49   What is ghee?

50   Briefly describe the following:
         chilli con carne; hash browns; clam chowder; sucotash.

51   Briefly describe pecan pie.

52   Name two Thai dishes.

51   What is an essential ingredient to many Thai dishes?

SHORT QUESTIONS — **ANSWERS**

1   to develop an understanding of the customs and styles of eating of other peoples; wider knowledge of food, cooking and ingredients

2   religious influences   *p302 PC*

3   alcohol and pork; Halal.   *p302 PC*

4   because the cow is a sacred animal   *p302 PC*

5   Hindus; Buddhists   *p302 PC*

6   e.g. ginger, cinnamon, turmeric, coriander, cumin, nutmeg

7   metagee   *p303 PC*

8   bananas

9   e.g. yams; sweet potatoes   *p303 PC*

10 e.g. almond chicken – stir fried chicken, almonds, onions, bamboo
     shoots, water chestnuts, mushrooms   *p305 PC*

11 true

12 all ingredients must be prepared in advance and ready to cook

13 soya beans

14 sesame seed

15 vine leaves with a rice based savoury stuffing; onion, garlic, rice,
     tomato purée, pine kernels, herbs   *p312 PC*

16 Baklava   *p313 PC*

17 seasoned cooked minced lamb dish with aubergine and tomato
           p267 PC

18 to extract the full flavour

19 3 hours

20 e.g. ginger; coriander; cumin; chilli   *p320 PC*

21 lentil or split pea purée

22 thick   *p321 PC*

23 a clay oven

24 tandoori

25 hot oven or grill

26 vegetable salad, peanut dressing;   *p326 PC*
     rice with chicken, bacon, vegetables and soya sauce *p327 PC*

27 more suitable for stir fry dishes

28 soya bean curd

29 vinegared rice   *p330 PC*

30 tempura   *p328 PC*

31 skewered, marinated meats or vegetables; grilled marinated good
     quality of strips of meat   *p329 PC*

32 sweet sherry; sesame seed oil; white vinegar; castor sugar *p329 PC*

33 fresh raw fish   *p330 PC*

34 thin pancakes; crisp thin pancakes; tortillas filled with spring
    mixture; tortillas rolled and filled; Mexican pancakes filled with
    meat   *pp333–334 PC*

35 chick peas; sesame seed paste   *p335 PC*

36 garlic; onions; lemon; paprika   *p335 PC*

37 tabbouleh   *p336 PC*

38 Morocco; Tunis; Algeria   *p338 PC*

39 semolina grain steamed over a stew or broth   *p338 PC*

40 only by steaming   *p338 PC*

41 milk products and meat kept separate in storage, preparation and
    serving. Also separate utensils and equipment must be used. Meat
    slaughtered according to Jewish law   *pp339–340 PC*

42 grated raw potato, onion and egg fried in cakes   *p340 PC*

43 plaited rich yeast bread   *p342 PC*

44 fried wafers of unleavened bread; baked fluffy batter with nuts and
    cinnamon   *pp342–343 PC*

45 lobster, squid, prawns, mussels, chicken, rice, onion, garlic,
    peppers, saffron, tomatoes, oil; all cooked together in a paella pan
                                                            p345 PC

46 sausage   *p346 PC*

47 by gently sweating them in fat or oil

48 a spice mixture

49 pure butter fat

50 hot spiced beef stew with beans in chilli sauce; raw, grated potato
    cakes with bacon; thick shellfish soup; lima beans, sweetcorn and
    bacon   *pp354–355 PC*

51 open tart filled with sweet pecan mixture   *p356 PC*

52 Thai fish cakes; mussaman curry   *p347 PC*
    barbequed tofu

53 Garlic mixture (Kru tium prig tai)   *p350 PC*

VEGETARIAN DISHES

CHAPTER 11

Read pp 357–384 of *Practical Cookery*, also vegetable and pulses
Chapter 12/pp 385–423.

SHORT QUESTIONS

1   Very briefly explain the difference between a vegan and a
vegetarian.

2   From what is soy sauce derived?

3   What is tofu?

4   What are crudités?
crude oils; raw vegetables; oriental spices

5   Match the following:

Ratatouille	a source of oil
Lentils	a vegetable dish
Allspice	a pulse
Sesame seed	a seasoning
Smetana	a colouring
Saffron	a dairy product

6   What is tvp?

7   Name six nuts.

8   Outline the method for cooking dried beans.

9   For what reasons do people become vegetarians?

10   List four vegetarian dishes suitable as a main course.

11   Name a dish using quorn.

12   Name a dish using tofu.

QUESTIONS IN DEPTH

1   a   Discuss the factors concerning vegetables that affect their
cooking times.

b   State the general rules for boiling vegetables, explain the reasons why some are started in cold water and others in boiling water and how the nutritive value is affected.

c   What is the difference between the preparation of runner beans and French beans?

d   What are the differences between the cooking for: fresh peas; frozen peas; French style peas; sugar peas (mange-tout)

2   a   Briefly describe three different ways of cooking cabbage. What is the effect of overcooking cabbage, or any green vegetable, in relation to its food value?

b   By which method of cookery is red cabbage usually cooked and what ingredients may be added?

c   What are the advantages of high speed steam cookers in relation to batch cookery?

d   State the quality and purchasing points of root and green vegetables and how they should be stored.

e   What is the difference between a vegetarian and a vegan?

SHORT QUESTIONS – ANSWERS

1   vegetarians and vegans do not eat fish, meat, poultry or game and vegans in addition do not consume dairy products, milk and eggs

p358 PC

2   soya beans

3   low fat bean curd made from soya beans

4   raw vegetables

5   ratatouille – a vegetable dish; lentils – a pulse; allspice – a seasoning; sesame seed – a source of oil; smetana – a dairy product; saffron – a colouring

6   textured vegetable protein derived from soya beans

7   e.g. walnuts; pecans; almonds; hazelnuts; peanuts; pistachios

8   pick and wash, soak for up to 24 hours (if necessary), drain off water, cover with fresh water, simmer gently with additional flavouring of vegetables and herbs.

9   e.g. religion, health, choice

10 e.g. bean goulash, Caribbean fruit curry, Cornish vegetable feast bake pie, vegetarian moussaka

11 Stir fry quorn   *p377 PC*

12 Warm tofu and asparagus salad   *p382 PC*

QUESTIONS IN DEPTH — **OUTLINE ANSWERS** _____

1   **a**   age; quality; freshness; size and type
    b   root vegetables in cold, green vegetables in boiling water
            minimum cooking time retains maximum flavour, food value,
            colour
    c   side strings removed from runner beans, cut in thin strips;
            French beans topped and tailed, cut into even strips
    d   fresh peas – varied cooking times according to age, freshness
            size
            frozen peas – consistent cooking time of short duration
            French style peas – cooked under cover with additional
            ingredients either on top of stove or in oven, thickened with
            beurre manié
            sugar peas (mange-tout) – topped and tailed, cooked and
            served in the pods

2   **a**   e.g. boiled or steamed (trim, shred, wash, cook for minimum
            time);
            stir fried; braised, with vegetables, herbs, stock
            overcooking lessens vitamin content
    b   by braising – with the addition of vinegar, apples etc.
    c   reduction in cooking time; retention of flavour; smaller
            quantities cooked as required during service
    d   root vegetables should be clean, firm, sound;
            green vegetables should be fresh, condition of leaves
            root – empty from sacks, store in bins, or racks
            green – store in a well ventilated, cool area
            salad – store in a cool area, preferably refrigerated
    e   a vegetarian does not eat any meat or fish but will eat dairy
            produce; vegans do not eat meat, fish or dairy produce

VEGETABLES AND PULSES

CHAPTER 12

Read pp 385–422 of *Practical Cookery*.

SHORT QUESTIONS

1   Vegetables which grow above the ground should be started in boiling salted water: true/false.

2   As a general rule the cooking of all root vegetables with the exception of new potatoes is started in cold salted water: true/false.

3   Suggest a suitable sauce for serving with the following.
     hot globe artichoke; cold globe artichoke

4   To cook a globe artichoke allow approximately:
     5–10 minutes; 10–15 minutes; 20–30 minutes; 40–45 minutes

5   Name the liquid in which artichoke bottoms are cooked.

6   Two types of artichoke are used in cookery. One is globe, name the other.

7   What is the current price of a globe artichoke?

8   What is the current price of a tin of artichoke bottoms?

9   How many pieces of asparagus are usually served per portion?
     2–3; 4–5; 6–8; 10–12

10 It is not necessary to wash asparagus before cooking: true/false.

11 Asparagus will cook in approximately:
     5 minutes; 10 minutes; 15 minutes; 20 minutes

12 Suggest two sauces for serving with hot asparagus.

13 Asparagus is only served hot: true false.

14 What is the approximate price of fresh asparagus per ½kg (1lb)?

15 What is an approximate price of frozen asparagus per ½kg (1lb)?

16   Young thin asparagus are known as . . .

17   The French name for egg-plant is . . .

18   What is the price of aubergines?

19   Could duxelle be used to stuff egg-plant? yes/no.

20   What is ratatouille?

21   Broccoli may be cooked and served as for any cauliflower recipe: true/false.

22   What is the price of fresh broccoli?

23   What is the price of frozen broccoli?

24   When cooking buttered carrots, how would you glaze them?

25   Vichy carrots should be cooked in the same way as buttered carrots: true/false.

26   What is the price of carrots?

27   What basic sauce would you use for carrots in cream sauce?
         velouté; suprême; hollandaise; béchamel

28   To cook braised celery allow approximately:
         1 hour; 2 hours; 3 hours; 4 hours

29   What is the price of twelve heads of fresh celery?

30   What is the price of twelve large tins of celery hearts?

31   The cooking liquor from braised celery is added to an equal amount of . . . or . . . in order to make the coating sauce.

32   ½kg (1lb) cabbage will yield:
         1–2 portions; 3–4 portions; 5–6 portions; 7–8 portions

33   What is the price of cabbage?

34   When cooking cabbage, state two factors which affect the vitamin content.

35   Suggest a suitable filling for braised stuffed cabbage.

36   What is Sauerkraut?
         braised cabbage; boiled white cabbage; German spring cabbage; pickled white cabbage

37   Suggest four different ways of serving cauliflower.

38   What is the price of a six-portion cauliflower?

39   Cauliflower polonaise is finished with:
         browned breadcrumbs, sieved hard-boiled eggs and chopped
         parsley; cheese sauce; breadcrumbs and cheese; butter,
         breadcrumbs and parsley

40   Suggest two suitable sauces for serving with seakale.

41   What is the price of seakale?

42   All variations for cooking and serving cauliflower may be used as
     for marrow: true/false.

43   What is the price of 20kg (40lb) marrow?

44   To prepare marrow Provençale you would add:
         chopped onion, garlic, tomatoes and parsley; chopped onion,
         garlic, pimento and parsley; chopped onion, mushrooms,
         parsley and garlic; chopped onion, garlic, mushrooms and
         pimento

45   1kg (2lb) spinach will yield:
         1 portion; 2 portions; 3 portions; 4 portions

46   Spinach is a vegetable that needs a minimum washing: true/false.

47   The time required to cook spinach is approximately:
         2 minutes; 5 minutes; 10 minutes; 15 minutes

48   What is the current market price of fresh spinach?

49   What is the current market price of frozen spinach?

50   Before cooking haricot beans they may be soaked overnight in
     cold water: true/false.

51   Approximately how much of the following would you add when
     cooking 1kg (2lb) haricot beans?
         carrot; onion; bacon trimmings

52   To cook corn on the cob, allow approximately:
         5 minutes; 10 minutes; 15 minutes; 30 minutes

53   What is the difference between fried onions and French fried
     onions?

54   What size onions would you select for braising?

55   What is the price of onions?

56   ½kg (1lb) of fresh peas in the pod will yield approximately . . . portions.

57   ½kg (1lb) of frozen peas will yield approximately . . . portions.

58   Which of the following would you use in preparing peas, French style?
       lettuce and button onions; lettuce and mushrooms;
       mushrooms and button onions; mushrooms and garlic

59   A mixture of peas and carrots is known as . . . style.

60   When preparing stuffed pimento, would you use red pimento or green pimento?

61   What is the difference between red and green pimentos?

62   The base of the stuffing used for stuffed pimento is:
       breadcrumbs; sausagemeat; mixed vegetables; rice

63   Salsify should be cooked in a blanc: true/false.

64   What is the price of salsify?

65   To remove the skins from tomatoes plunge them into boiling water for approximately:
       1–2 seconds; 3–4 seconds; 5–6 seconds; 9–10 seconds
     What factor determines the length of time?

66   What ingredients are added to tomatoes to make tomato concassé?

67   What is the current market price of English tomatoes?

68   What is the current market price of imported tomatoes?

69   1kg (2lb) leeks prepared for braising will yield approximately:
       1 portion; 2 portions; 3 portions; 4 portions

70   When preparing pease pudding it is usual to use:
       frozen peas; tinned peas; split green peas; split yellow peas

71   Is it more efficient to cook pease pudding on top of the stove or in the oven?

72   What ingredients in addition to peas would you add to pease pudding to improve the flavour?

73   Which of the following is used in a dish of mixed vegetables?
       swedes, turnips, haricot beans, peas; swedes, turnips
       mushrooms; carrots, turnips, mushrooms; carrots, turnips,
       peas, French beans

74 What are pulses?

75 In what three forms are pulses available?

76 Pulses are a good source of protein and carbohydrate: true or false?

77 Name three pulses.

78 Name three types of dried peas.

79 Name three types of lentils.

80 Name three dishes each prepared from a different pulse.

81 If a pulse is to be soaked before cooking, what is the procedure?

82 When and why should salt be added when boiling a pulse?

83 What are puy and dahl?

SHORT QUESTIONS — **ANSWERS**

1	true	*p388 PC*
2	true	*p388 PC*
3	hollandaise; vinaigrette	*p390 PC*
4	20–30 minutes depending on size	*p390 PC*
5	blanc	*p391 PC*
6	Jerusalem	
7	current market price	
8	current market price	
9	6–8 according to size	*p392 PC*
10	false, it is important to thoroughly wash them, especially the tips as they may contain sandy soil	*p392 PC*
11	15 minutes, according to thickness	*p392 PC*
12	maltaise; hollandaise	*p392 PC*
13	false, it is also popular served cold	*p392 PC*
14	current market price	
15	current market price	

16 sprue

17 aubergine   *p392 PC*

18 current market price

19 yes   *p394 PC*

20 cooked mixture of marrow, aubergine, tomato, onion and
   peppers   *p393 PC*

21 true

22 current market price

23 current market price

24 by evaporating the water in which they were cooked and tossing
   them in butter over fierce heat   *p395 PC*

25 true   *p395 PC*

26 current market price

27 béchamel   *p396 PC*

28 approx two hours according to age and size   *p400 PC*

29 current market price

30 current market price

31 jus lié or demi-glace   *p400 PC*

32 3–4 portions   *p397 PC*

33 current market price

34 overcooking; addition of soda   *p397 PC*

35 sausagemeat   *p398 PC*

36 pickled white cabbage   *p399 PC*

37 e.g. with cream sauce, mornay, butter   *p402 PC*

38 current market price

39 browned breadcrumbs, sieved hard-boiled eggs, parsley   *p402 PC*

40 melted butter, hollandaise   *p402 PC*

41 current market price

42 true   *p402 PC*

43 current market price *p404 PC*

44 chopped onion, garlic, tomatoes and parsley *p405 PC*

45 2 portions *p405 PC*

46 false, it can be very gritty *p405 PC*

47 approximately 2–5 minutes according to age and size

48 current market price

49 current market price

50 true

51 100g (4oz) carrot, 100g (4oz) onion, 100g (4oz) bacon trimmings

52 15 minutes according to freshness *p407 PC*

53 French fried are deep fried onion rings; fried onions are shallow fried *pp408/409 PC*

54 medium size *p409 PC*

55 current market price

56 2 portions *p410 PC*

57 8 portions *p410 PC*

58 lettuce and button onions *p410 PC*

59 à la flamande or Flemish style *p411 PC*

60 red

61 the red are fully ripe

62 rice *p411 PC*

63 true *p411 PC*

64 current market price

65 9–10 seconds – the riper the tomato the less time

66 chopped shallots, fat

67 current market price

68 current market price

69 4 portions *p415 PC*

70   split yellow peas   *p416 PC*

71   in the oven   *p416 PC*

72   studded onion, carrot, bacon scraps   *p416 PC*

73   carrots, turnips, peas, French beans   *p417 PC*

74   dried seeds of plants which form pods   *p420 PC*

75   fresh, dried, canned   *p420 PC*

76   true   *p420 PC*

77   e.g. peas; beans; lentils   *p421 PC*

78   e.g. yellow split; chick; blue (marrowfat)   *p421 PC*

79   e.g. yellow; red; brown   *p421 PC*

80   e.g. bean salad, lentil and cider loaf, spiced chick peas   *p421 PC*

81   amply cover with water and keep in a cold place   *p422 PC*

82   when the pulse is almost cooked. If added at the beginning of
cooking it can toughen the pulse   *p422 PC*

83   puy are dark French lentils which retain shape when cooking. Dhal
is the Hindu word for dried peas and beans   *p422 PC*

POTATOES

CHAPTER 13

Read pp 423–436 of *Practical Cookery*.

SHORT QUESTIONS

1   State the nutritional content of potatoes.

2   Approximately how many portions can be obtained from ½kg (1lb) of old potatoes, and new potatoes?

3   Even-sized boiled potatoes will cook in approximately:
        10 minutes; 15 minutes; 20 minutes; 30 minutes

4   How are parsley potatoes cooked?
        boiling; roasting; sautéing; frying; steaming

5   Riced potatoes are a mixture of half potatoes half rice: true/false.

6   Why are butter or margarine and warm milk added to mashed potatoes?

7   What ingredients can be added to mashed potatoes in order to make a variation?

8   What ingredients are added to dry mashed potato in order to make duchess potatoes?

9   Why are duchess potatoes dried after piping, before brushing them with egg-wash?

10   What are brioche potatoes made from:
        mashed potatoes; duchess potatoes; sauté potatoes; baked jacket potatoes

11   Why should croquette potatoes be passed through flour, egg and crumbs before being deep fried?

12   What is added to duchess potatoes to make marquis potatoes?
        onion; cheese; tomato

13   What is the best way to pre-cook potatoes for sauté potatoes?
        boil in jacket; steam in jacket; peel and boil; peel, slice and steam

14 When preparing Lyonnaise potatoes, allow two parts onion to one part potatoes: true/false.

15 Game chips should be cooked in cool fat: true/false.

16 When giving chipped potatoes their 'first fry' the temperature of the fat should be:
     100°C; 120°C; 140°C; 165°C

17 After frying and before serving, chipped potatoes may be lightly seasoned with salt: true/false.

18 When preparing savoury potatoes use two parts of potato to one part of onion: true/false.

19 How long does it take to cook four portions of savoury potatoes?
     20 minutes; 45 minutes; 1 hour; 1½ hours

20 Fondant potatoes are even-sized, brushed with butter or margarine and cooked in stock in the oven: true/false.

21 Roast potatoes should be cooked in a hot oven 230°C–250°C: true/false.

22 Both château potatoes and fondant potatoes are cooked in stock in the oven: true/false.

23 Noisette potatoes are turned with a small kitchen knife: true/false.

24 Parisienne potatoes should be finished by rolling in a little meat glaze: true/false.

25 Delmonico potatoes are cooked in white stock: true/false.

26 Boiling is the only efficient method of cooking new potatoes: true/false.

27 Parmentier potatoes should be deep fried: true/false.

28 Potatoes Anna, like savoury potatoes, should contain a proportion of finely sliced onion: true/false.

QUESTIONS IN DEPTH

1   a   What is the approximate yield from ½kg (1lb) of old and new potatoes?
     b   Describe the making of duchess potato and explain how three variations can be made.

   c Explain why fondant potatoes are so called and how they are prepared.

   d Describe the preparation and cooking of savoury potatoes and with what dish they are frequently offered.

SHORT QUESTIONS — **ANSWERS**

1   approx 20% starch, a small amount protein (under skin), vitamin C

2   old potatoes, 3 portions; new potatoes, 4 portions

3   20 minutes

4   boiling or steaming

5   false, all potato

6   to enrich them

7   cheese, cream etc.   *p425 PC*

8   egg yolks and butter or margarine

9   to reduce the risk of spoiling the shape when brushing with egg wash

10   duchess potatoes

11   to hold the duchess mixture together, to stop fat penetration and to form a crisp golden brown surface after frying

12   tomato

13   steam in jacket

14   false

15   false, hot fat

16   165°C

17   true

18   false, four parts potato to one part onion

19   1½ hours

20   true

21   true

22   false, only fondant potatoes; chateau potatoes are cooked in fat

23 false, a noisette cutter is used

24 true

25 false, they are cooked in milk

26 false, they can be steamed

27 false, they should be shallow fried

28 false, there is no onion in potatoes Anna

QUESTIONS IN DEPTH – OUTLINE ANSWERS _____

1   **a**   old potatoes, 3 portions; new potatoes, 4 portions   *p424 PC*
     b   potatoes are mashed, addition of egg yolk and butter, piped,
           firmed, egg washed and browned   *p426 PC*
           e.g. croquettes, moulded, pané, deep fried
     c   even sized potatoes are brushed with melted butter then
           cooked in stock in the oven. The stock is absorbed by the
           potatoes giving them a soft, melting (fondant) quality
     d   thin sliced potatoes, onions, stock, seasoning
           oven baked, served with roast lamb   *p432 PC*

PASTRY

CHAPTER 14

Read pp 437–567 of *Practical Cookery*.

SHORT QUESTIONS

1   What pastry is used for Cornish pasties and fruit pies?
     puff; rough puff; flaky; short

2   What is the usual proportion of fat to flour for short pastry?
     1 part fat to 1 part flour; 1 part fat to 2 parts flour; 1 part fat
     to 3 parts flour; 1 part fat to 4 parts flour

3   When being mixed, short pastry should be handled firmly and well
     kneaded: true/false.

4   Give one possible reason for each of the following faults in short
     pastry:
     hard; soft-crumbly; blistered; soggy; shrunken

5   When making puff pastry, is strong flour or soft flour used?

6   What is the usual proportion of fat to flour for puff pastry?
     1 part fat to 1 part flour; 1 part fat to 2 parts flour; 1 part fat
     to 3 parts flour; 1 part fat to 4 parts flour

7   List four ways of adding fat to flour.

8   Why is it essential to rest the paste between the various stages of
     making puff pastry?

9   What is the cost of the following?
     flour; lard; butter; margarine; cooking fat

10   What causes the lift or lightness in puff pastry?

11   Why is an acid such as lemon juice added when making puff
     pastry?

12   Give one reason for each of the following faults in puff pastry:
     not flaky; fat oozes out; hard; shrunken; soggy; uneven
     rise

13 What is the usual proportion of fat to flour for rough puff pastry?
    1 part fat to 1 part flour; 1 part fat to 2 parts flour; 3 parts fat
    to 4 parts flour; 3 parts fat to 5 parts flour

14 It is best to use sugar paste immediately after it has been made:
    true/false.

15 What are the prices of the following?
    castor sugar; granulated sugar; loaf sugar; icing sugar

16 Which paste is used for flans and fruit tartlets?
    short; rough puff; sugar

17 Baking powder is used in making suet paste: true/false.

18 What is the usual proportion of suet to flour in suet paste?
    1 part suet to 1 part flour; 1 part suet to 2 parts flour; 1 part
    suet to 3 parts flour; 1 part suet to 4 parts flour

19 Give one reason for each of the following faults in suet paste:
    heavy-soggy; tough; lumps of suet

20 What is hot water paste used for?

21 At what temperature should hot water paste be used?
    hot; cold; warm

22 What is the approximate number of eggs per ½ litre (1pt) of
    choux paste
    4; 8; 12; 16

23 What is the price of eggs?

24 Name three items prepared from choux paste.

25 Give one reason for each of the following faults in choux paste:
    greasy and heavy; soft – not aerated

26 How many scones should a mixture using 200g (½lb) flour base
    yield?

27 What is added to a basic scone mixture to make fruit scones?
    currants; raisins; angelica and cherries; sultanas

28 Give four variations to basic small cake mixture.

29 Give one reason for each of the following faults in sponges:
    close texture; holey; sunken; white spots on surface

30 A Genoese sponge contains a fat or oil: true/false.

31 What is the proportion of fat to flour in Genoese?
    1 part fat to 1 part flour; 1 part fat to 2 parts flour; 1 part fat
    to 3 parts flour; 1 part fat to 4 parts flour

32 What ingredient is added to the basic mixture for Genoese in
    order to make chocolate Genoese?

33 What should be the flavour of gâteau moka?

34 Give one reason for each of the following faults in yeast dough:
    close texture; uneven texture; coarse texture; wrinkled; sour;
    broken crust; white spots on crust

35 Flour for making bread and rolls should be a strong flour and
    should be warmed: true/false.

36 What happens when a yeast dough is proved?

37 What two extra ingredients are added to a basic dough in order to
    make bun dough?

38 What is the price of yeast?

39 Give three examples of goods made from bun dough.

40 What should doughnuts be fried in:
    cool fat; moderately hot fat; hot fat; very hot fat

41 Savarin paste contains yeast: true/false.

42 What two ingredients are added to savarin paste in order to make
    rum babas?

43 What ingredients are used in preparing a syrup for soaking babas?

44 Which of the following is the odd one out and why?
    baba; savarin; meringue; marignan

45 Name six fruits or combination of fruits suitable for making into a
    fruit pie.

46 Which ingredient is missing from the following list for the filling
    for a treacle tart: syrup or treacle, lemon juice, water, . . . ?

47 Baked apple dumplings are usually made with:
    rough puff paste; sugar paste; short paste; puff paste

48 What is the price of cooking apples?

49 What two ingredients are put into the centre of an apple before
    covering it with pastry for a baked apple dumpling?

50 Which of the following are added to Dutch apple tart?
      currants; raisins; sultanas; dates

51 What is the traditional finish for apple flan?
      red glaze; yellow jelly; icing sugar; apricot glaze

52 Should cherries in a cherry flan be stoned: yes/no.

53 Fruit flans should be cooked in a cool oven; hot oven; moderately hot oven; fierce oven

54 What may be placed as a layer on the base of a rhubarb flan?

55 What is the price of rhubarb?

56 Name three types of fruit flan for which the flan case is baked blind.

57 Is the flan case 'blind' for a banana flan: yes/no.

58 What is the price of bananas?

59 Is it usual to put a layer on the base of a banana flan: yes/no. If so, what can be used?

60 What is the difference between a strawberry tartlet and a strawberry barquette?

61 What is the price of fresh strawberries in season?

62 What is the price of frozen strawberries?

63 What is the distinctive flavouring in the filling of bakewell tart?

64 What jam should be used in the base of a bakewell tart?
      apricot; strawberry; raspberry; red plum

65 What is the main filling in a lemon meringue pie?

66 What is the price of a dozen lemons?

67 What item could be made from the following ingredients?
      100g (4oz) butter or margarine; 2 eggs; 100g (4oz) castor sugar; 1 lemon

68 What is the difference between a jam turnover and a jam puff?

69 Which paste is used for cream horns?
      short paste; sugar paste; flaky paste; puff paste

70 Is a little jam placed in the bottom of a cream horn after cooking and before filling with cream: yes/no.

71 Cream horns should be baked in:
        hot oven; moderately hot oven; cool oven; very hot oven.

72 What is the reason for sprinkling some puff pastry goods with icing sugar and returning them to a hot oven at the last stage of cooking?

73 What is the English for mille-feuilles?

74 What is the literal translation of mille-feuilles?

75 What is the traditional filling for mille-feuilles?

76 Which of the traditional fillings for mille-feuilles is sometimes varied because of popular taste?

77 What is the term given to the traditional decorative finish for mille-feuilles?

78 Which of the following would be the odd one out as a filling for jalousie:
        mincemeat; frangipane; jam; apple

79 Which filling is used for a gâteau Pithiviers?
        marzipan; mincemeat; cooked rice; frangipane

80 To make palmiers it is essential to use good puff pastry: true/false.

81 How can you make two palmiers into a tea pastry?

82 Suggest two sauces suitable for serving with mince pies.

83 How many bouchées can be obtained from puff pastry using 200g (½lb) flour?

84 Bouchées should be cooked on greased, dampened baking sheets: true/false.

85 What is the name given to large bouchées?

86 What variation in flavour in addition to chocolate is used for éclairs?

87 What happens to the fondant glaze on éclairs if it is overheated?

88 What ingredient may be sprinkled on cream buns before they are baked?

89 How are cream buns finished before service?

90 What are profiteroles?

91 In how many sizes may profiteroles be made, and for what purpose?

92 When serving profiteroles filled with cream as a sweet, which sauce is usually offered?

      jam; raspberry; vanilla; chocolate

93 What are pieces of choux paste the size of a walnut cooked in deep fat called?

94 Suggest three fruits or combinations of fruits suitable for steamed fruit suet pudding.

95 What is the approximate cooking time for a steamed fruit pudding?

      1 hour; 1½ hours; 2½ hours; 3 hours

96 Give the basic quantities of the following ingredients for six portions of steamed sponge pudding:

      castor sugar; eggs; baking powder; margarine; flour; milk

97 Suggest six variations for a steamed sponge pudding together with a sauce that can be offered with each.

98 Why is a soufflé pudding so called?

99 Soufflé pudding should be cooked in a bain-marie in a hot oven: true/false.

100 What is the dominant flavour of soufflé milanaise?

101 What is the top layer on queen of puddings?

      breadcrumbs; baked custard; meringue; thin sheets of puff pastry

102 What thickness are apple rings cut for apple fritters?

      ½cm (¼in); 1cm (½in); 1½cm (¾in); 2cm (1in)

103 In a fairly hot fat, apple fritters require approximately:

      2 minutes on each side; 3 minutes on each side; 4 minutes on each side; 5 minutes on each side

104 What sauce is usually offered with apple fritters?

      custard; apricot; syrup; orange

105 What fruits are suitable for serving as fritters?

106 Complete this list of quantities of ingredients for pancake batter:

      100g (4oz) flour; milk; pinch of salt; egg; melted butter or margarine

107 Suggest three ways of serving pancakes.

108 Suggest a suitable stuffing for a baked apple.

109 List six fresh fruits suitable for fruit salad.

110 What ingredient added to milk causes it to coagulate or clot?

111 What is the name of the sweet made by the process in question 110 and what other ingredients should be added?

112 Which spice is generally used to sprinkle on the sweet in question 111?
        clove; cinnamon; nutmeg; ginger

113 Suggest four suitable fruits for making fruit fool.

114 Suggest four suitable fruits for inclusion in a fruit trifle.

115 How much sugar is needed for meringue using four egg whites?

116 As the aim when cooking meringues is to cook them without colouring they should be cooked in the slowest oven possible: true/false.

117 Name four important points to be observed when whipping egg whites.

118 Why do egg whites increase in volume when whipped?

119 What is a vacherin?
        two meringues joined by a ball of ice cream; two meringues joined by whipped cream; a special mould for shaping meringue; a round case of meringue shell

120 What is the name of the sweet with a base of sponge, a layer of ice cream and a coating of meringue, browned in the oven?

121 What is a fruit compote?

122 What is the correct finish for a jam omelet?

123 Name four types of simple milk puddings.

124 What is a fruit condé?

125 Name four fruits suitable for preparing as a condé.

126 What glaze is used to finish a condé?

127 What is the price of rice?

128   What proportion of eggs to milk is required for a baked egg custard?

> 4 size 3 eggs – 1 litre (2pts) milk; 6 size 3 eggs – 1 litre (2pts) milk; 8 size 3 eggs – 1 litre (2pts) milk; 10 size 3 eggs – 1 litre (2pts) milk

129   What fruit is used in a bread and butter pudding?

> dates; figs; sultanas; apricots

130   It is not necessary to cook a bread and butter pudding in a bain-marie provided the oven is cool enough: true/false.

131   What sweet can be made from stale bread?

132   What sweet with an egg custard base is made using diced sponge and fruit?

133   What name is given to the sweet in question 132 when served cold?

134   Add the quantities to this list of ingredients for cream caramel:

> ½ litre (1pt) milk; sugar; eggs; vanilla
> caramel – sugar; water

135   Cream caramels should be cooked in a bain-marie in:

> a hot oven; a fierce oven; a cool oven; a moderately hot oven

136   What is bavarois?

137   Suggest six varieties of bavarois.

138   What is pastry cream?

> whipped sweetened cream for filling pastries; a basic pastry preparation of thick custard; bavarois mixture in pastry cases; mock cream used as a substitute for fresh cream

139   Which of the following ice creams is prepared as a sorbet?

> vanilla; chocolate; lemon; coffee

140   The correct ice cream used for pear Belle Hélène is:

> vanilla; chocolate; strawberry; coffee

141   What is a sabayon sauce?

142   Suggest a suitable hot sweet for serving accompanied by a sauce sabayon.

143   What is zabaglione?

144 What are the two basic categories of petit fours?

145 List four examples of petit fours in each of the two categories mentioned in question 144.

146 What type of sugar is used in making langues de chat?
   brown; castor; granulated; icing

147 What can be used to shape cornets after they are cooked?

148 What is praline?

149 How is praline made?

150 What is praline used for?

QUESTIONS IN DEPTH

1 **a** What is the difference between a strong and soft flour? Which would be the more suitable for puff pastry and short pastry and give reasons why.
   b **i** Give the proportion of fat to flour for short pastry and sugar pastry.
      ii List four possible reasons for faults in short pastry.
      iii Name four examples for the use of short pastry.
   c **i** Explain the principles of making successful puff pastry.
      ii Suggest six possible reasons for faults.
   d State ingredients and method for making choux pastry and give four examples of its use.

2 **a** **i** State ingredients and method for making a Victoria sandwich
      ii Give five reasons for possible faults when making.
      iii How does the making of a Genoese sponge differ?
   b Give ingredients and method for making a basic bread dough.
   c What is yeast, what is its food value and what points should be observed when using it? Give four examples of products made from bun dough.

3 **a** Name and briefly describe four sweets that can be prepared using cooking apples.
   b Suggest six fruits suitable for fresh fruit salad and describe the method of preparation and service.
   c State the ingredients and method for a fruit fool, and indicate three suitable fruits.

d Give the procedure for stiffly whipping egg whites, the method for making meringues and briefly describe and name three sweets that can be produced using meringue.

SHORT QUESTIONS — **ANSWERS** _____

1 short

2 1 : 2

3 false, it should be handled lightly

4 excessive rolling; fat; water; oven temperature; handling *p514 PC*

5 strong

6 1 : 1

7 rubbing in; creaming; lamination; boiling

8 otherwise the pastry will shrink and when cut and baked the products will be misshapen *p515 PC*

9 current market price (find this out)

10 mainly due to air trapped in during the folding process and the steam pushing the layers apart *p515 PC*

11 helps to strengthen the gluten content in the flour, making it more pliable and better able to retain the layers of fat during rolling

12 e.g. rolling; folding; flour; stretching; oven temperature; fat distribution *p515 PC*

13 3 : 4

14 false, it should be allowed to rest and relax in a cool place

15 current market price (find this out)

16 sugar

17 true

18 1 : 2

19 e.g. cooking temperature; handling; insufficiently chopped
  p517 PC

20 raised meat pies *p116 PC*

21   warm

22   8

23   current market price (find this out)

24   éclairs; cream buns; profiteroles

25   basic mixture; insufficient beating   *p518 PC*

26   8

27   sultanas

28   e.g. cherry or coconut cakes, raspberry buns, Queen cakes
      p552 PC

29   e.g. underbeating; adding flour; oven temperature; movement of
      moulds during baking; beating

30   true

31   1 : 2

32   cocoa or chocolate powder

33   coffee

34   e.g. proving; kneading; water; yeast, quantity of yeast; second
      stage proving; covering   *p490 PC*

35   true

36   the yeast being a form of plant life, grows on the sugar and in the
      liquid and warmth of the dough. The sugar causes fermentation,
      produces gas (carbon dioxide) and alcohol in small bubbles. When
      oven heat is applied the dough rises   *p488 PC*

37   eggs and butter

38   current market price

39   e.g. fruit buns, Bath buns, Chelsea buns   *pp502–3 PC*

40   hot fat or oil

41   true

42   currants, rum

43   sugar; water; lemon; bay leaf; cinnamon; coriander   *p505 PC*

44   meringue – does not contain yeast

45 e.g. apple, damson, blackberry and apple   *p519 PC*

46 white breadcrumbs

47 short paste

48 current market price

49 sugar, cloves

50 sultanas

51 apricot glaze

52 yes

53 hot oven

54 pastry cream

55 current market price

56 e.g. strawberry; raspberry; tinned peach   *p527 PC*

57 yes

58 current market price

59 yes, pastry cream

60 tartlet – round; barquette – boat shaped

61 current market price

62 current market price

63 frangipane or almond cream

64 raspberry

65 lemon curd

66 current market price

67 lemon curd

68 shape   *p532 PC*

69 puff paste

70 yes

71 hot

72 to give them an appetising, shiny appearance known as a glaze

73   cream slice

74   thousand leaves

75   apricot jam; pastry cream

76   whipped cream instead of pastry cream

77   feathering or feather icing

78   jam

79   frangipane

80   false, trimmings, provided they are rested, are adequate

81   join them together with whipped cream

82   custard; brandy butter

83   12

84   true

85   vol-au-vent

86   coffee

87   goes dull

88   chopped almonds

89   sprinkle with icing sugar

90   small cream buns made from choux paste

91   pea size – consommé; double pea size for stuffing and garnish; half cream bun size for serving with chocolate sauce

92   chocolate

93   fritters   *p542 PC*

94   e.g. rhubarb, apple, rhubarb and apple   *p543 PC*

95   1½ hours

96   100g (4oz) castor sugar; 2 eggs; 10g (½oz) baking powder; 100g (4oz) margarine; 150g (6oz) flour; few drops of milk   *p460 PC*

97   e.g. vanilla – custard sauce; orange – orange sauce   *p460 PC*

98   because of its light aerated consistency

99   true

100   lemon

101   meringue

102   ½cm (¼in)

103   5 minutes each side

104   apricot

105   apple; banana; pineapple

106   1 egg, 250ml (½pt) milk, 10g (½oz) fat and oil   *p462 PC*

107   e.g. with jam; apple; orange   *p462 PC*

108   sultanas, raisins or chopped dates   *p479 PC*

109   e.g. apples; pears; pineapple; oranges; strawberries   *p480 PC*

110   rennet

111   junket; sugar, spice

112   nutmeg

113   e.g. rhubarb; raspberry   *p482 PC*

114   e.g. peaches; pears   *p444 PC*

115   200g (8oz)

116   true

117   e.g. fresh eggs, no specks of yolk, clean bowl and whisk   *p463 PC*

118   because air is incorporated during the whipping process

          p463 PC

119   a round case of meringue shell

120   baked Alaska

121   assorted stewed fruit

122   sprinkle with sugar and caramelise   *p126 PC*

123   rice; semolina; sago; tapioca

124   cooked fruit on a base of cooked rice coated with a
      glaze   *p485 PC*

125   e.g. peach; pear; banana; pineapple

126   apricot glaze

127   current market price

128   6 size 3 eggs – 1 litre milk

129   sultanas

130   false, cooking in a bain-marie in a moderate oven ensures a slow
       oven heat which is essential   *p445 PC*

131   bread pudding   *p468 PC*

132   Cabinet pudding   *p446 PC*

133   Diplomat pudding

134   100g (4oz) sugar, 4 eggs, 3–4 drops vanilla
       caramel – 100g (4oz) sugar, 125ml (¼pt) water   *p447 PC*

135   moderately hot oven

136   a lightly gelatine set cold sweet of milk, eggs, cream and
       flavouring   *p449 PC*

137   e.g. vanilla; chocolate; strawberry   *p449 PC*

138   basic pastry preparation of thick custard   *p454 PC*

139   lemon

140   vanilla

141   a sauce made from egg yolks, sugar and white wine   *p453 PC*

142   e.g. apple charlotte

143   the Italian version of a sabayon, usually made with Marsala
       wine

144   dry, glazed

145   e.g. langues de chat; sablés; stuffed dates; sugar dipped grapes
                                                              p563 PC

146   icing

147   cream horn moulds

148   crushed basic preparation of browned nuts and sugar   *p476 PC*

149   browned nuts into caramel stage sugar, cooled, crushed

150   used for flavouring many sweets e.g. cakes, gâteaux, ice
       creams

QUESTIONS IN DEPTH – OUTLINE ANSWERS _____

1   a   the proportion of gluten proteins (gliadin and glutenin): low
        proportion in soft flour, high proportion in strong flour

                                                                p508 PC

        strong – tougher dough assists retention of fat when rolling
                  puff pastry
        soft   – assists soft biscuity texture in pastry (the fat breaks
                  down the shorter gluten strands)

    b   i   short – 2 flour : 1 fat   *p514 PC*
             sugar – 5 flour : 3 fat   *p517 PC*
        ii   e.g. excess water; fat content and mixing; incorrect mixing;
             over handling   *p514 PC*
        iii e.g. pies, Cornish pasties

    c   i   good basic dough, texture of dough and fat equal, rolling
             and method of folding, resting   *p515 PC*
        ii   incorrect fat texture, oven temperature, water, flour,
             insufficient resting, handling   *p516 PC*

    d   water, sugar and fat boiled, cooled, eggs thoroughly beaten in
                                                                p518 PC

        e.g. gnocchi, éclairs, fritters

2   a   i   Victoria sandwich – 100g (4oz) each fat, sugar, flour,
             baking powder, 2 eggs
             Cream fat and sugar, beat in eggs, fold in flour *p555 PC*
        ii   e.g. beating and mixing incorrectly, quantities, incorrect
             oven temperature
        iii Genoese sponge – eggs, sugar beaten over heat, flour
             folded in, fat is added as a liquid   *p556 PC*

    b   flour, yeast, liquid, fat
        warmed flour, creamed yeast, fermenting, kneading, proving
                                                                p488 PC

    c   a plant life; contains protein, vitamin B
        e.g. warm not hot temperature, minimum salt, liquid at blood
        heat, 32°C (90°F)
        e.g. hot cross buns, Chelsea buns   *p490 PC*

3   a   apple pie – peeled sliced cooking apples, sweetened, flavoured,
        covered short pastry *p667 PC*; apple flan *p671 PC*; apple
        charlotte *p627 PC*; apple fritters *p627 PC*

    b   e.g. ripe dessert apples, pears, oranges, cherries, strawberries;
        fruit peeled and neatly cut, mixed in stock syrup or natural
        syrup with minimum of handling   *illustration p481 PC*

c   puréed fruit, sugar, cream e.g. apple, raspberry   *p482 PC*

d   eggs fresh, no yolk, clean bowl and whisk piping on silicone
    paper, very low oven temperature, cool   *p463 PC*
    e.g. meringue with whipped cream, strawberry
    vacherin   *p464 PC*

SAVOURIES, COCKTAIL SAVOURIES, SANDWICHES

CHAPTER 15

Read pp 568–581 of *Practical Cookery*.

SHORT QUESTIONS

1   What is the difference between angels on horseback and devils on horseback?

2   With what are prunes stuffed in the preparation for devils on horseback?

3   Which mushrooms are selected for mushrooms on toast?
    button; open

4   What is the cost of button mushrooms and open mushrooms?

5   Suggest two ways of serving curried shrimps or prawns as a savoury.

6   What are the prices of prepared shrimps and prepared prawns?

7   What are the ingredients of a croque monsieur?
    ham, cheese, toast; bacon, cheese, toast; ham, mushroom, toast; bacon, mushroom, toast

8   What price are:
    smoked haddock; kipper; smoked salmon

9   When preparing soft roes on toast, the roes need not be floured: true/false.

10   What is the price of soft roes?

11   How would you cook soft roes?
    grilling; baking; poaching; frying; boiling

12   What is Scotch woodcock?
    a game bird from Scotland; a colloquial term for tripe as prepared in Glasgow; scrambled eggs on toast garnished with anchovies and capers; a game pâté first produced in Balmoral

13 What type of bacon is used for haddock and bacon savouries?
      back; gammon; streaky; collar

14 Suggest two variations that can be made to a basic creamed haddock on toast.

15 Which cheese is used for Welsh rarebit?
      Stilton; Caerphilly; Wensleydale; Cheddar

16 Suggest four seasonings or flavourings that can be used when making Welsh rarebit.

17 A buck rarebit is a Welsh rarebit with the addition of:
      bacon; mushroom; ham; poached egg

18 What is the base of a cheese soufflé mixture?

19 When making cheese soufflé, how many egg whites would you add to the following mixture?
      25g (1oz) butter; 125ml (¼pt) milk; salt; 15g (¾oz) flour; 3 egg yolks; 50g (2oz) grated cheese; cayenne

20 Approximately how long would the mixture in question 22 take to cook in a hot oven?
      5 minutes; 15–20 minutes; 10–12 minutes; 25–30 minutes

21 When a soufflé is cooked, if not required immediately it should be stood in a bain-marie and kept in the top of a hot plate: true/false.

22 What two ingredients are added to puff pastry in order to make cheese straws?

23 Suggest an interesting filling for a savoury flan.

24 What pastry would be used for a savoury flan?

25 Name eight food items which could be served at a cocktail party.

26 What does the word canapé indicate?
      specific garnish; Russian cake; cushion for food; sliced sausage

27 Suggest six bouchée fillings.

28 Suggest four different types of bread suitable for sandwiches.

29 Suggest an interesting variety of six sandwich fillings.

30 Suggest four examples of combination fillings for sandwiches.

31   Suggest five different seasonings that are suitable for varying the flavour of sandwiches.

32   Which of the following would you sprinkle on to a dish of sandwiches?
     chopped parsley; watercress; mustard and cress; shredded lettuce

33   What is a toasted sandwich?

34   Give two examples of popular toasted sandwiches.

35   Two slices of hot buttered toast with a filling of lettuce, grilled bacon, sliced hard boiled egg, slice of chicken and mayonnaise is known as:
     savoury toasted sandwich; book-maker sandwich; jumbo sandwich; club sandwich

36   What is the name given to an underdone minute steak between two slices of hot buttered toast?

37   What are the following?
     double decker sandwich; treble decker sandwich

38   Give two examples for each:
     double decker; treble decker

39   Give a brief description of an open sandwich.

40   Suggest four interesting varieties of open sandwich.

41   Open sandwiches are traditionally prepared with fresh bread or toast?

42   List six hygiene factors which must be taken into account when preparing sandwiches.

43   List four materials that can be used for packing sandwiches.

QUESTIONS IN DEPTH

1   a   Name and describe three savouries using cheese.
    b   Name and describe three savouries in which items are wrapped in bacon, skewered and grilled.
    c   What are Scotch woodcock, Welsh rarebit and buck rarebit?

2   a   What are cocktail or reception canapés and what size should they be? Suggest six cold and six hot items.

   b   Suggest six different fillings suitable for savoury bouchées.

   c   Name six types of bread from which sandwiches can be made. Give examples of fillings for three single items and three combinations. What seasonings can be added to flavour sandwich fillings?

SHORT QUESTIONS – **ANSWERS** _____

1	oysters; prunes	*p570 PC*
2	chutney	
3	open	
4	current market price (find this out)	
5	on toast; in a bouchée	
6	current market price (find this out)	
7	ham, cheese, toast	*p572 PC*
8	current market price (find this out)	
9	false	
10	current market price (find this out)	
11	shallow fried or grilled	
12	scrambled eggs on toast garnished with anchovies and capers	
13	streaky	
14	grated cheese, pickled walnut	
15	Cheddar	
16	e.g. mustard, cayenne, Worcester sauce	*p573 PC*
17	poached egg	
18	Béchamel	
19	3 egg whites	
20	approx 25 minutes	
21	false, it must be served immediately otherwise there is a risk of it sagging	
22	grated cheese, cayenne	

23   e.g. mushroom and prawn; courgette and tomato

24   short

25   chicken bouchées; assorted canapés; game chips; celery sticks
     spread with cheese; etc.   *p579 PC*

26   cushion for food   *p583 PC*

27   e.g. mushroom, prawn   *p579 PC*

28   e.g. white; wholemeal; rye; caraway seed

29   e.g. ham; beef; egg; tuna fish; tomato; cucumber

30   e.g. fish and lettuce; cheese and tomato   *p580 PC*

31   e.g. mayonnaise, mustard, chutney   *p580 PC*

32   mustard and cress

33   savoury filling between two slices of hot freshly buttered toast
                                                                 p581 PC

34   e.g. ham; bacon   *p581 PC*

35   club sandwich   *p581 PC*

36   bookmaker sandwich   *p581 PC*

37   toasted and untoasted bread using three or four slices of bread
     with different fillings in between each layer

38   e.g. ham and tomato; crispy bacon, lettuce, tomato

39   a buttered slice of bread generously covered with either meat, fish,
     egg, vegetable   *p581 PC*

40   e.g. smoked salmon, lettuce; potted shrimps, slice of lemon;
     shredded lettuce, slice hard boiled egg, cucumber, mayonnaise
                                                                 p581 PC

41   fresh bread

42   e.g. clean protective clothing, hair covered, no nail varnish or
     finger jewellery, hands and finger-nails scrubbed clean, disposable
     gloves; clean utensils and work surfaces; bread, spreads and fillings
     fresh, kept refrigerated before and after making up. If to be kept,
     store in a cool place
     avoid cross-contamination e.g. fish, meat, eggs; all handlers to be
     trained in basic food and personal hygiene; ultra-violet fly killer

43   clingwrap; greaseproof paper; polystyrene containers;
       polypropylene

QUESTIONS IN DEPTH – **OUTLINE ANSWERS** _____

1   **a**   e.g. cheese fritters – choux paste with cheese, deep fried;
            p575 PC
            cheese soufflé – light, baked cheese mixture   *p575 PC*
       b   e.g. Canapé Diane – chicken livers *p731 PC*; angels on
            horseback – oysters *p727 PC*; devils on horseback – prunes
            p727 PC
       c   scrambled egg on toast, garnished *p732 PC*; seasoned cheese,
            toast *p732 PC*; seasoned cheese mixture on toast with a
            poached egg *p733 PC*

2   **a**   small food items, hot or cold served prior to main meals, size –
            a comfortable mouthful
            cold – e.g. smoked salmon, sliced hard boiled egg on brown
            bread
            hot – e.g. shrimp bouchées, mini-pizzas   *p579 PC*
       b   e.g. mushrooms with chopped herbs in cream sauce;
            diced vegetables in fromage frais   *p579 PC*
       c   e.g. white; wholemeal; rye; granary   *p580 PC*
            e.g. ham; cheese; sardine
            e.g. tuna fish and cucumber; cheese, apple and chutney
            e.g. mayonnaise, mustard, chutney   *p580 PC*

CULINARY TERMS

Read pp 582–586 of *Practical Cookery*.

SHORT QUESTIONS

1 What do you understand by the term offal?

2 What are giblets?
   poultry offal; fish fillets; type of bacteria; a rice dish

3 What is French for 'in the style of' as used in menus?

4 'À la carte' and 'carte du jour' are two common terms; explain 'à la carte'.

5 What are bacteria?
   micro-organisms; harmful rays; small insects; minute animals

6 Give three explanations of the term 'bain-marie'.

7 What are bean sprouts?

8 Which is used during roasting?
   breading; blanc; basting; ballottine

9 'Blanching' is a common culinary term with five meanings; define blanching in five ways.

10 What are crudités?

11 How do bouchées and vol-au-vents differ?

12 Match the following:
   brunoise   thin strips
   paysanne   ½cm (¼in) dice
   macédoine   small dice
   julienne   thin rounds, triangles or squares

13 A canapé is a dish cover: true/false.

14 Carbohydrates consist of three groups; name all three.

15   What is the value of calcium to the diet?
        prevents skin disease; builds bones and teeth; provides
        vitamin C; gives energy

16   What is the culinary meaning of 'clarification'?

17   *Clostridium perfringens* are food poisoning bacteria; where are
      they found?

18   What is understood by 'correcting' when related to a soup or a
      sauce?

19   Explain the difference between a darne and a tronçon.

20   Deglaze means to serve on ice: true/false.

21   What is duxelle?
        chopped mushrooms and onions – cooked; chopped
        mushrooms and shallots – cooked; chopped mushrooms and
        breadcrumbs – cooked; chopped mushrooms and minced
        meat – cooked

22   Give two examples of emulsions used in the kitchen.

23   How are the two emulsions in your answer to question 22
      used?

24   When are petits fours served?

25   Explain the difference between a blanquette and a fricassée.

26   What is garam masala?

27   A liaison is for:
        tiering; turning; thickening; trussing

28   Give three different examples of the use of the term 'to glaze'.

29   What is the difference between mirepoix and macédoine?

30   Monosodium glutamate is used to increase flavour: true/false.

31   If the term 'native' is on the menu what would it signify?
        a dish for locals; okra fingers; English oysters; a speciality

32   What is a pulse?
        a dried pod vegetable; a savoury rice; a vegetable soup; a
        dried fruit

33   The term 'refresh' is frequently used in cookery; what does it
      mean?

34 If working in the pastry what could you prove?

35 What is *salmonella* and where is it found?

36 What is *staphylococcus* and where is it found?

37 What is the culinary meaning of 'to sweat'?

SHORT QUESTIONS — **ANSWERS**

1 inner organs of animals e.g. heart, liver, etc.

2 poultry offal

3 à la

4 dishes prepared to order and priced individually

5 micro-organisms

6 e.g. containers of water   *p5823 PC*

7 young shoots of dried beans

8 basting

9 make white; retain colour; remove skin; make limp; cook without colour   *p582 PC*

10 pieces of raw vegetables served as an appetiser

11 bouchées are smaller in size

12 brunoise – small dice; paysanne – thin, neat shapes; macédoine – ¼in dice; julienne – thin strips

13 false, it is a cushion of bread for hot or cold foods   *p583 PC*

14 sugar; starch; cellulose

15 builds bones and teeth

16 to make clear; as in consommé, jelly

17 in the soil, vegetables and meat

18 adjusting; seasoning; consistency; colour

19 darne – slice of round fish on bone, e.g. salmon; tronçon – slice of flat fish on bone, e.g. turbot

20 false, it means to swill out a pan in which food has been cooked

21   chopped mushrooms and shallots – cooked

22   e.g. mayonnaise; hollandaise

23   e.g. salad dressing; warm sauce served with various foods e.g. fish

24   with coffee after a meal

25   blanquette – the meat is cooked in stock from which a white sauce is made; fricassée – the food is cooked in the white sauce

26   a ready prepared mixture of spices

27   thickening e.g. a velouté soup

28   to colour; to finish pastries; to finish vegetables   *p584 PC*

29   mirepoix – roughly cut vegetables; macédoine – neatly cut cubed vegetables or a mixture e.g. fruit salad

30   true

31   English oysters

32   dried pod vegetable   *p585 PC*

33   make cold under running water

34   yeast dough

35   food poisoning bacterium found in meat and poultry   *p585 PC*

36   food poisoning bacterium found in the human throat and nose, also in septic cuts   *p586 PC*

37   to cook in fat under a lid without colour

MULTIPLE CHOICE QUESTIONS

1 'Mise en place' means:
> clearing up afterwards; preparing in advance; replacing items used; returning food to store

2 Which joint of beef is most suitable for salting?
> shin; silverside; thick flank; sirloin

3 To boil rice allow approximately how long?
> 5 minutes; 15 minutes; 30 minutes; 1 hour

4 Which of the following is prepared from baked jacket potatoes?
> fondant potatoes; macaire potatoes; duchess potatoes; croquette potatoes

5 What is a mandolin used for?
> dicing; chopping; slicing; mincing

6 Espagnole is the basic sauce used for:
> roast gravy; tomato sauce; piquant sauce; suprême sauce

7 A tronçon is:
> a fillet of fish; a slice of flat fish on the bone; steak from a round fish; a cutlet of fish

8 What is jus lié?
> thin gravy; meat juice; thickened gravy; brown sauce

9 An egg custard can curdle during cooking because:
> too many eggs have been used; inaccurate amount of sugar used; too great a degree of heat; inferior quality eggs used

10 In which of the following potato dishes is the potato sieved?
> château; lyonnaise; duchesse; fondante

11 Approximately how many bouchées should ½kg (1lb) puff paste yield?
> 12; 24; 36; 48

12 After use, an omelet pan is cleaned by:
> plunging into hot water; cleaning with steel wool; rubbing with an abrasive powder; wiping with a clean cloth

13   What is apple pie usually covered with:
        puff pastry; crumble; short pastry; flaky pastry

14   The term meunière means:
        shallow fried; grilled; deep fried; crumbed and fried

15   Which of the following is a basic sauce?
        béchamel; anchovy; suprême; chaud-froid

16   Which of the following is an oily fish?
        herring; halibut; hake; haddock

17   Fish stock should simmer for how long?
        20 minutes; 40 minutes; 60 minutes; 90 minutes

18   Beef olives are cooked by:
        boiling; braising; frying; steaming

19   Junket is made from:
        sweet milk and gelatine; sweet milk and cornflour; sweet milk
        and riceflour; sweet milk and rennet

20   To produce 4¼ litres (1 gallon) of beef stock use:
        400g (1lb) of bones; 2kg (4lb) of bones; 5kg (10lb) of
        bones; 6kg (12lb) of bones

21   Choucroûte is made with:
        cauliflower; kale; sea-kale; cabbage

22   A noisette is cut from which joint of lamb?
        shoulder; leg; loin; neck

23   A salamander is used for:
        grilling; boiling; roasting; steaming

24   The proportion of sugar to whites of egg for meringue is:
        1 white to 50g (2oz) sugar; 1 white to 75g (3oz) sugar;
        1 white to 100g (4oz) sugar; 1 white to 125g (5oz)
        sugar

25   Osso buco is made using:
        shoulder of lamb; shoulder of veal; knuckle of lamb; knuckle
        of veal

26   A dish Condé is made using:
        semolina; rice; sago; tapioca

27   Prunes are used in:
        devils on horseback; Scotch woodcock; Welsh rarebit

28 A chicken cut resembling a toad is called:
   spatchcock; capilotade; grenouille; ballottine

29 A Gâteau Pithiviers in addition to puff pastry has:
   apricot jam, marzipan and icing sugar; royal icing, almond paste and apricot jam; apricot jam, frangipane and icing sugar; apricot jam, royal icing and marzipan

30 Macaire potatoes finished with grated cheese and cream are known as:
   Delmonico; Byron; dauphine; marquise

31 Poulet à la king contains:
   beef, demi-glace and red wine; chicken, chicken velouté and sherry; lamb, jus-lié and rice; veal, mushrooms and tomato sauce

32 Gelatine is added to bavarois:
   after adding the cream; when heating the milk; when the custard is cold; when the custard is hot

MULTIPLE CHOICE QUESTIONS — ANSWERS _____

1 preparing in advance

2 silverside

3 15 minutes

4 macaire

5 slicing

6 piquant sauce

7 slice of flat fish on the bone

8 thickened gravy

9 too great a degree of heat

10 duchesse

11 12

12 wiping with dry clean cloth

13 short pastry

14 shallow fried

15 béchamel

16 herring

17 20 minutes

18 braising

19 sweet milk and rennet

20 2kg (4lbs) of bones

21 cabbage

22 loin

23 grilling

24 1 white to 50g (2oz) sugar

25 knuckle of veal

26 rice

27 devils on horseback

28 spatchcock

29 apricot jam, frangipane and icing sugar

30 pommes Byron

31 chicken, chicken velouté and sherry

32 when the custard is hot

MIXED QUESTIONS

1   Name two typical British dishes using stewing lamb.

2   Which cuts from the carcass of lamb could be used for grilling?

3   What is the term for vegetables cut into thin strips?

4   A bouquet garni usually consists of:
onions, carrots, celery, leek; sage, onion, parsley, leek;
parsley, bayleaf, thyme, celery; celery, leek, bayleaf, rosemary

5   The approximate imperial equivalent of 1 litre is . . . ?

6   What does the culinary term to 'sweat' mean?

7   What is the name of the small item of equipment on which kebabs are pierced?

8   Name three British tea pastries.

9   Name three French tea pastries.

10 List the points to be considered when correcting a cream soup.

11 Name four herbs used in cooking.

12 It is better to overseason than underseason: true/false.

13 Melon is usually served as a . . . course.

14 List four vegetables suitable for braising.

15 Suggest an interesting selection of eight suitable sweet dishes for lunch or dinner.

16 Fried potatoes when served are covered with a lid: true/false.

17 Which of the following is the odd one out and why:
cream horns, eccles cakes, jam tarts, cream slice

18 Give a brief description of:
Welsh rarebit; Scotch woodcock; Irish stew

MIXED QUESTIONS – ANSWERS

1   e.g. Irish stew; Lancashire hotpot

2   cutlets; loin chops; chump chops

3   julienne

4   parsley, bayleaf, thyme, celery

5   1¾–2pts

6   to gently cook in fat without colouring

7   skewer

8   e.g. Chelsea buns, Bakewell tarts, Eccles cakes

9   e.g. Éclairs, Marignans, Palmiers

10 consistency; temperature; colour; seasoning; texture

11 e.g. thyme, bayleaf, parsley, sage

12 false, under-seasoning can be corrected, over-seasoning cannot

13 first

14 onions, leeks, celery, endives

15 e.g. fresh fruit salad; fruit flan; cream caramels; Charlotte russe; chocolate gâteau; lemon meringue pie; meringue Chantilly; profiteroles and chocolate sauce

16 false, because the steam created by the heat being contained by the lid will soften the crispness of the fried potatoes

17 jam tarts – made with short pastry, the other three are all made from puff pastry

18 toasted cheese on toast; scrambled eggs on toast garnished with capers, anchovies; lamb or mutton stew thickened with potato, leek, celery, onion